FOR ORGANS, PIANOS & ELECTRONIC KEYBOARDS

E-Z PLAY® TODAY

280

Dolly Parton

Cover Photo: Andrew Putler / Redferns / Retna Ltd.

ISBN 978-1-4234-2911-1

HAL•LEONARD® CORPORATION

7777 W. BLUEMOUND RD. P.O. BOX 13819 MILWAUKEE, WI 53213

Visit Hal Leonard Online at
www.halleonard.com

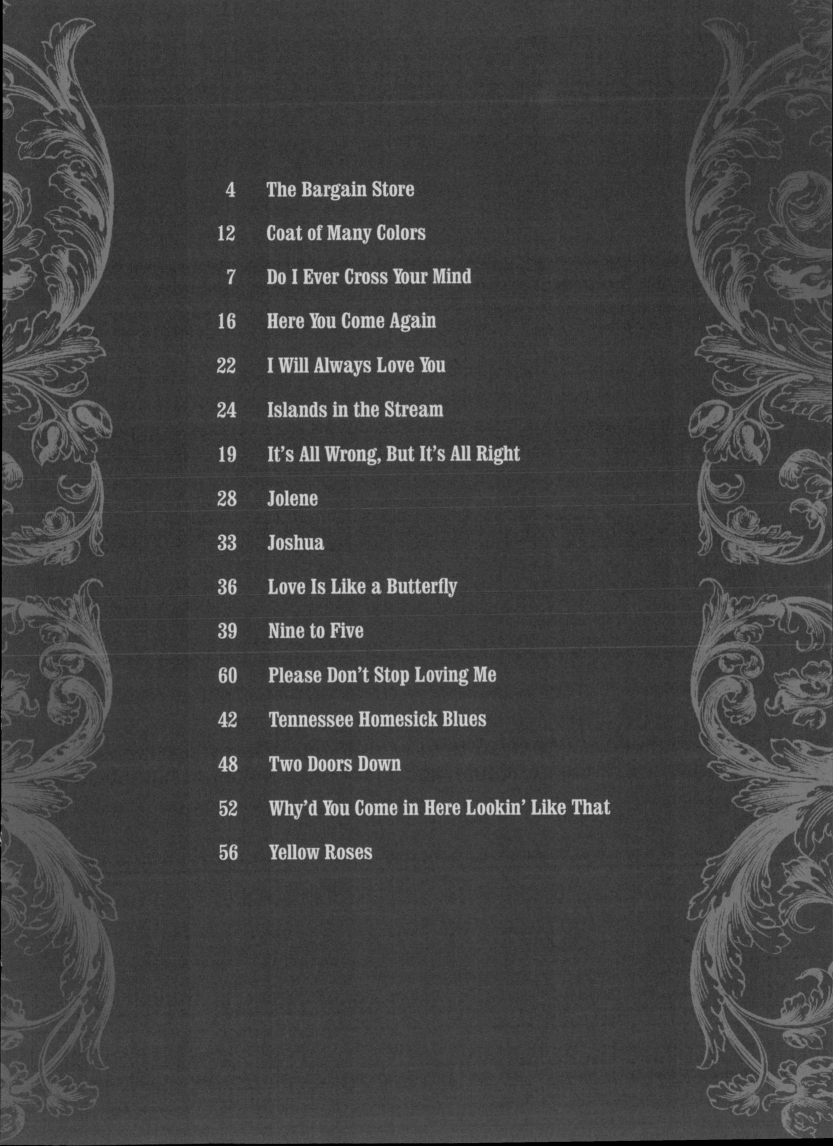

The Bargain Store

Registration 4
Rhythm: Country Swing or Fox Trot

Words and Music by
Dolly Parton

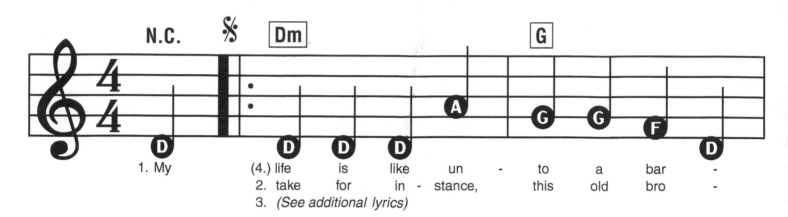

1. My (4.) life is like un - to a bar -
2. take for in - stance, this old bro -
3. *(See additional lyrics)*

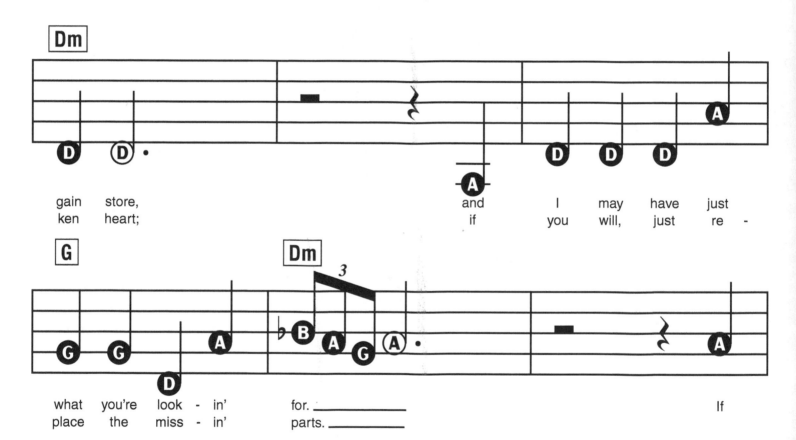

gain store,
ken heart;

and I may have just
if you will, just re -

what you're look - in' for. _____
place the miss - in' parts. _____

If

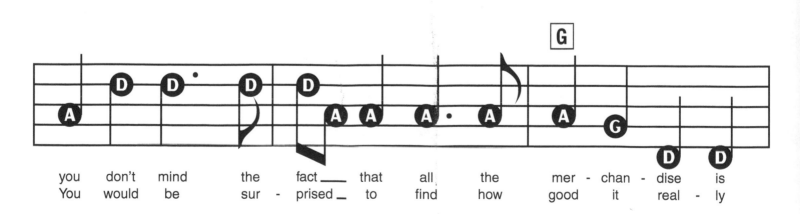

you don't mind the fact ___ that all the mer - chan - dise is
You would be sur - prised ___ to find how good it real - ly

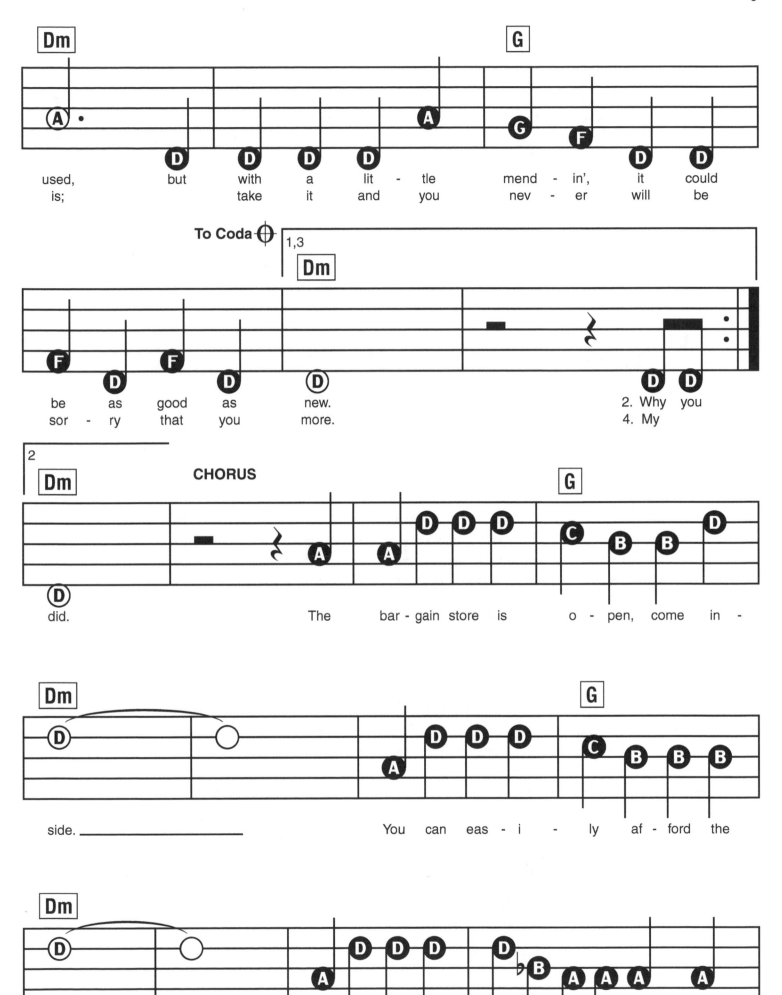

6

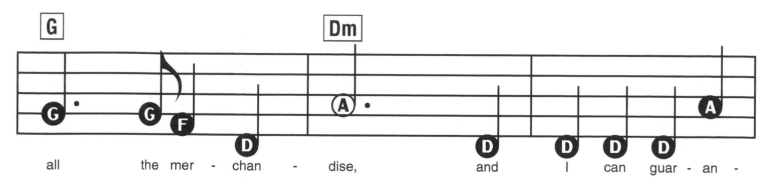

all   the mer - chan - dise,   and   I   can   guar - an -

D.S. al Coda
(Return to %
Play to ⊕ and
Skip to Coda)

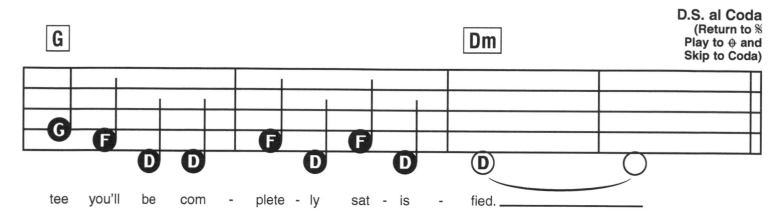

tee   you'll   be   com - plete - ly sat - is - fied. _____

CODA

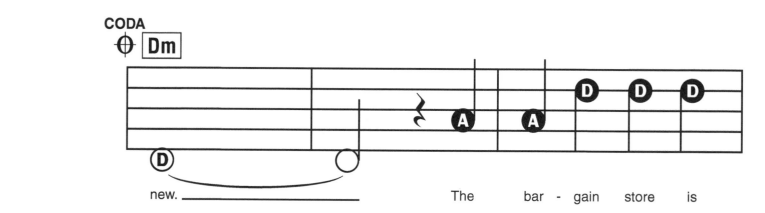

new. _____   The   bar - gain   store   is

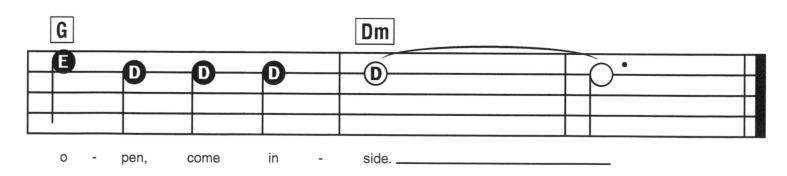

o - pen,   come   in - side. _____

Additional Lyrics

3. Take these old used memories from the past,
   And these broken dreams and plans that didn't last.
   I'll trade them for a future; I can't use them anymore.
   I've wasted love, but I still have some more.

Do I Ever Cross Your Mind

Registration 8
Rhythm: Country Swing or Fox Trot

Words and Music by
Dolly Parton

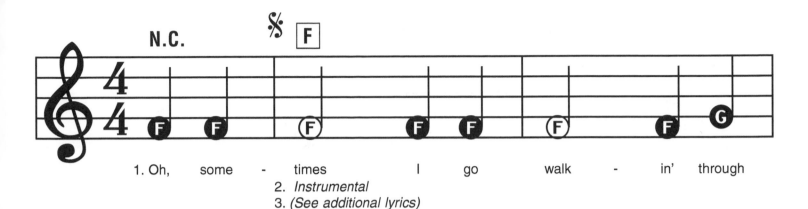

1. Oh, some - times I go walk - in' through
2. *Instrumental*
3. *(See additional lyrics)*

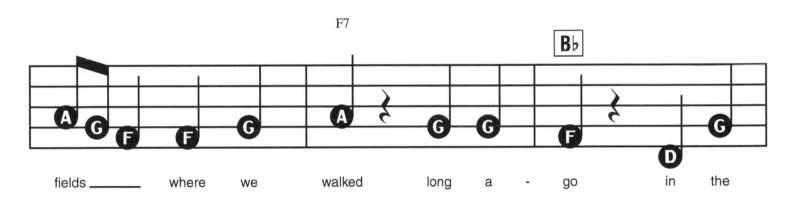

fields _____ where we walked long a - go in the

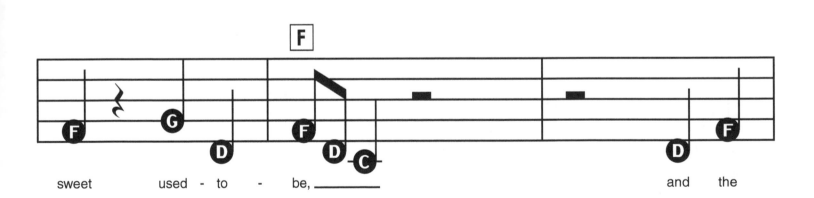

sweet used - to - be, _____ and the

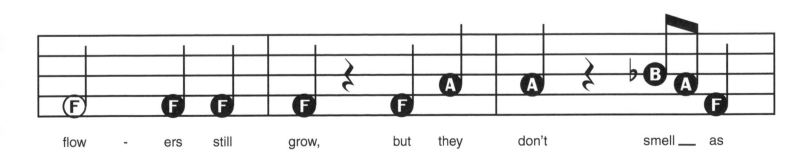

flow - ers still grow, but they don't smell ___ as

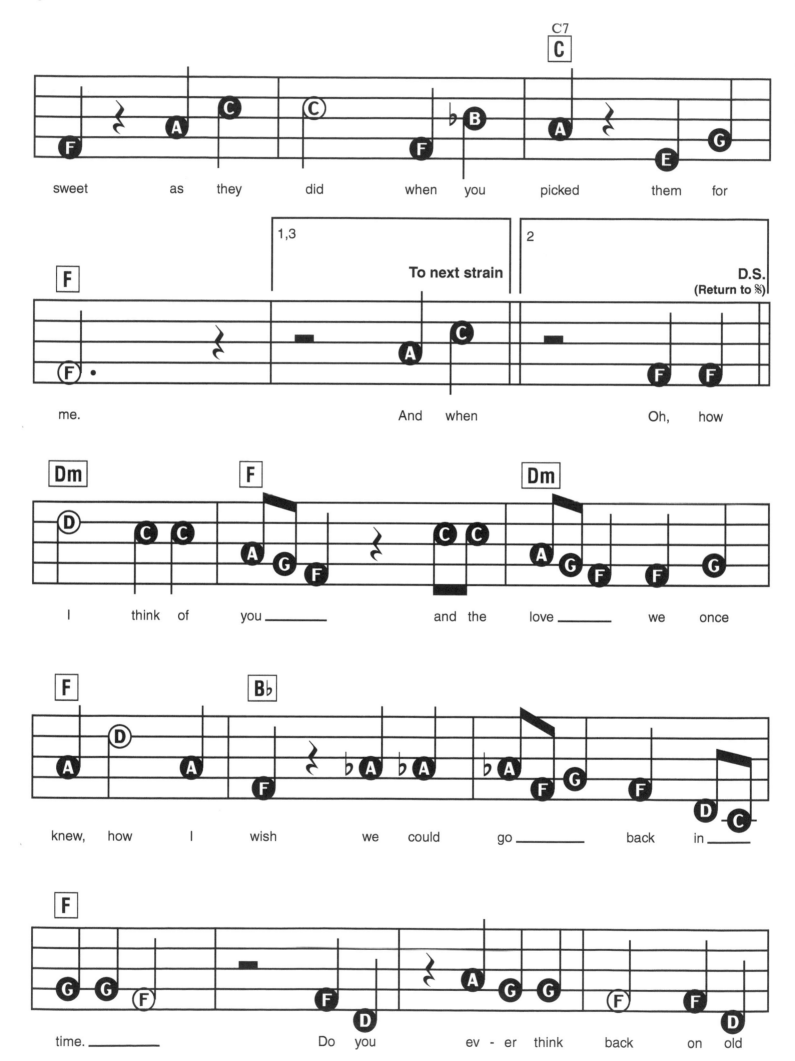

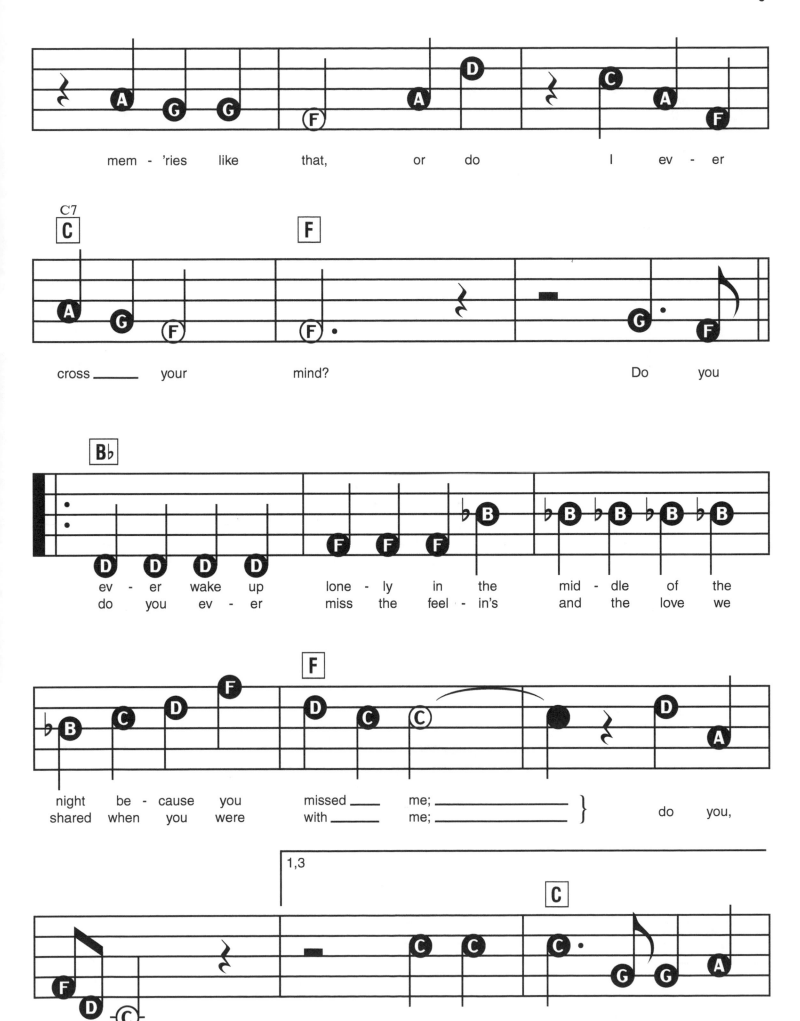

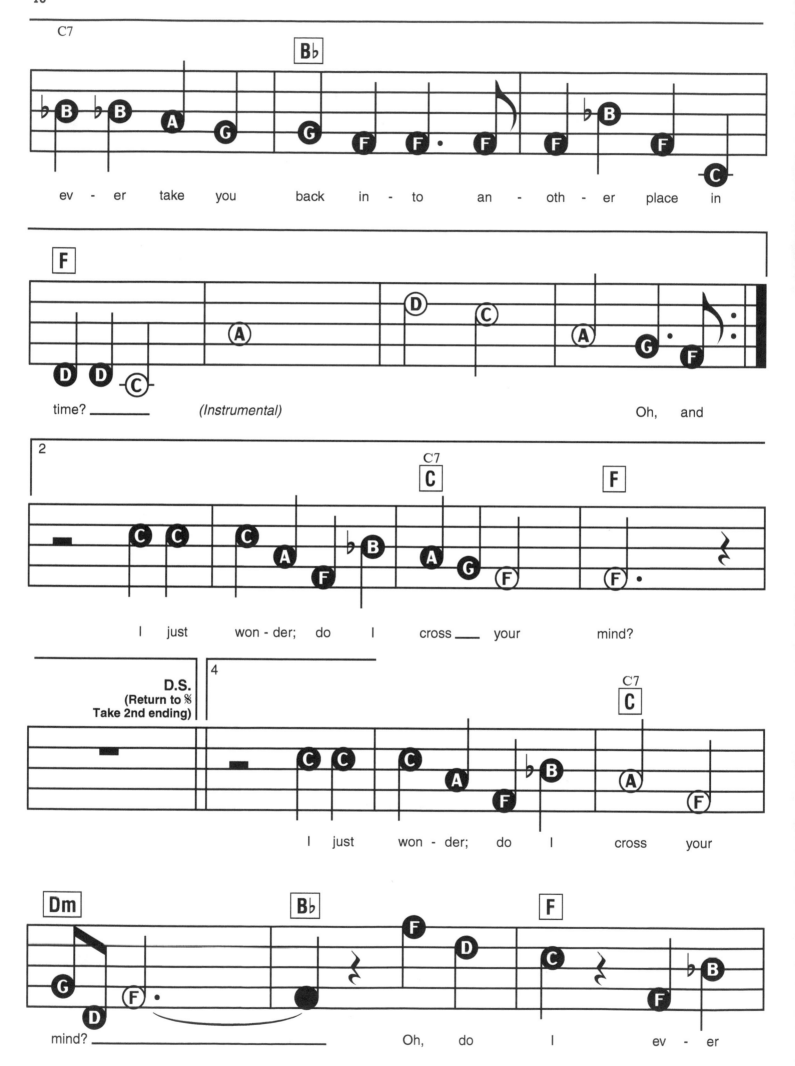

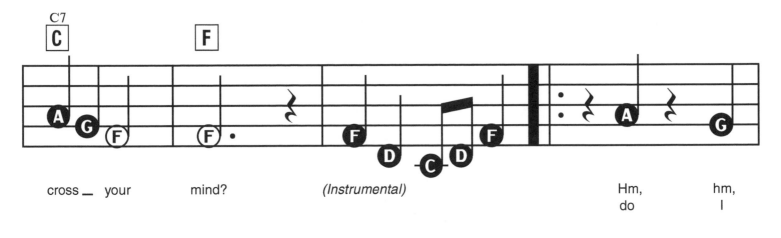

cross _ your mind?   *(Instrumental)*   Hm,   hm,
do   I

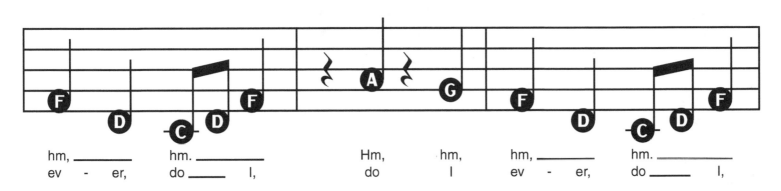

hm, _____ hm. _____   Hm,   hm,   hm, _____ hm. _____
ev - er,   do ___ I,   do   I   ev - er,   do ___ I,

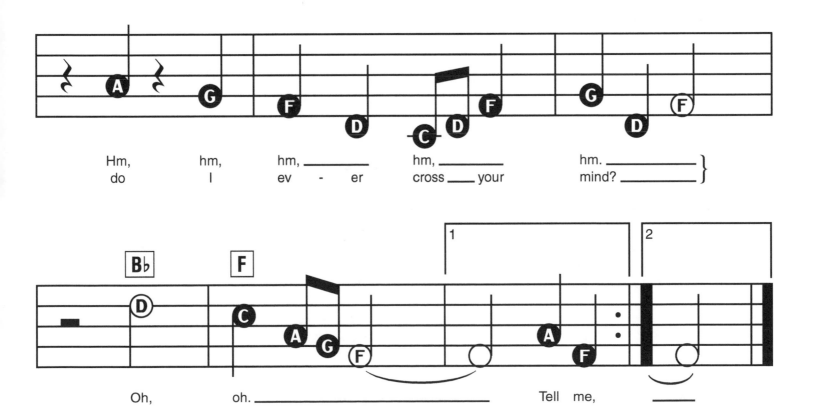

Hm,   hm,   hm, _____ hm, _____ hm. _____
do   I   ev - er   cross ___ your   mind? _____

Oh,   oh. _____   Tell me,   _____

Additional Lyrics

3. Oh, how often I wish that again I could kiss
   Your sweet lips like I did long ago,
   And how often I long for those two lovin' arms
   That once held me so gentle and close.

Coat of Many Colors

Registration 2
Rhythm: Country Swing or Fox Trot

Words and Music by
Dolly Parton

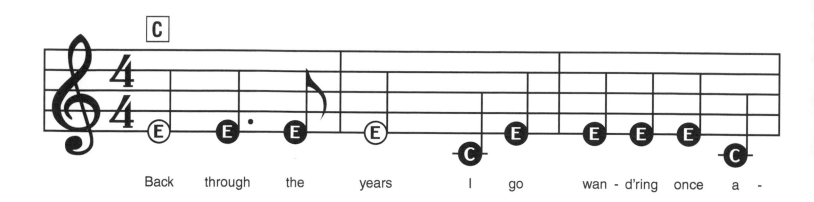

Back through the years I go wan - d'ring once a -

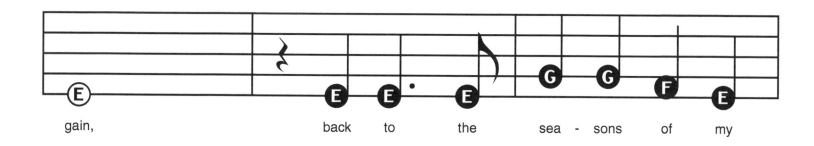

gain, back to the sea - sons of my

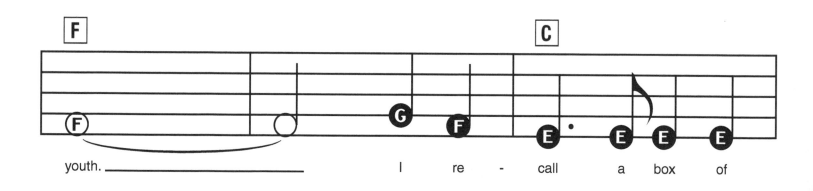

youth. _____ I re - call a box of

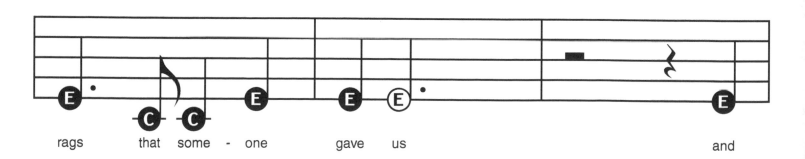

rags that some - one gave us and

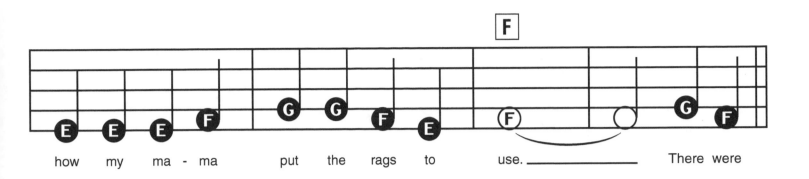

how my ma - ma put the rags to use. _____ There were

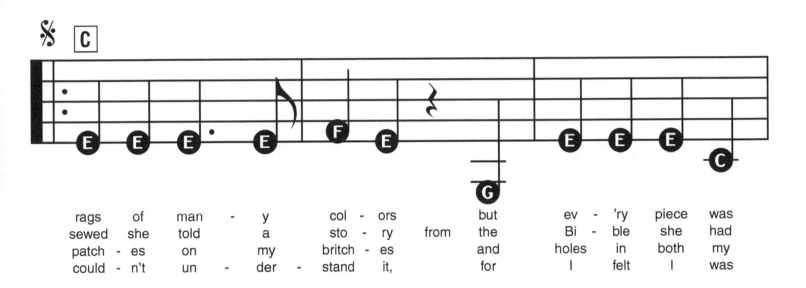

rags	of	man -	y	col - ors		but	ev -	'ry	piece	was
sewed	she	told	a	sto - ry	from	the	Bi -	ble	she	had
patch - es	on	my	britch - es	and		holes	in	both	my
could - n't	un - der -	stand	it,	for		I	felt	I	was

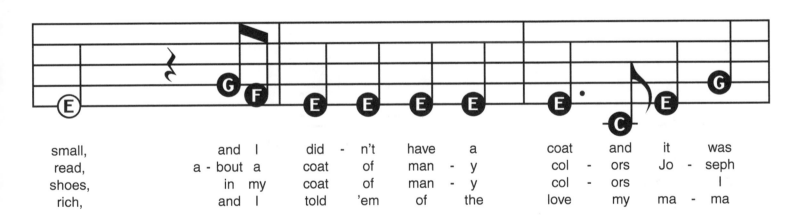

small,		and I	did - n't	have	a	coat	and	it	was
read,		a - bout a	coat	of	man - y	col - ors	Jo -	seph
shoes,		in my	coat	of	man - y	col - ors		I
rich,		and I	told	'em	of	the	love	my	ma - ma

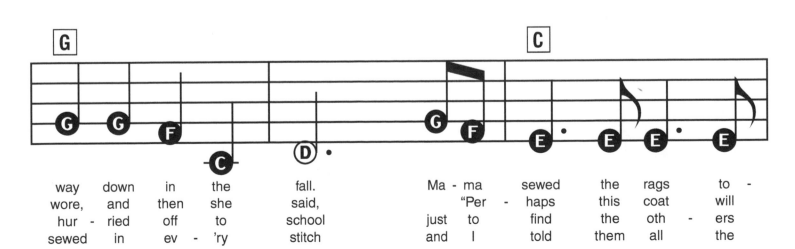

way	down	in	the	fall.	Ma - ma	sewed	the	rags	to -
wore,	and	then	she	said,	"Per - haps	this	coat	will
hur - ried	off	to	school	just	to	find	the	oth - ers
sewed	in	ev - 'ry	stitch	and	I	told	them	all	the

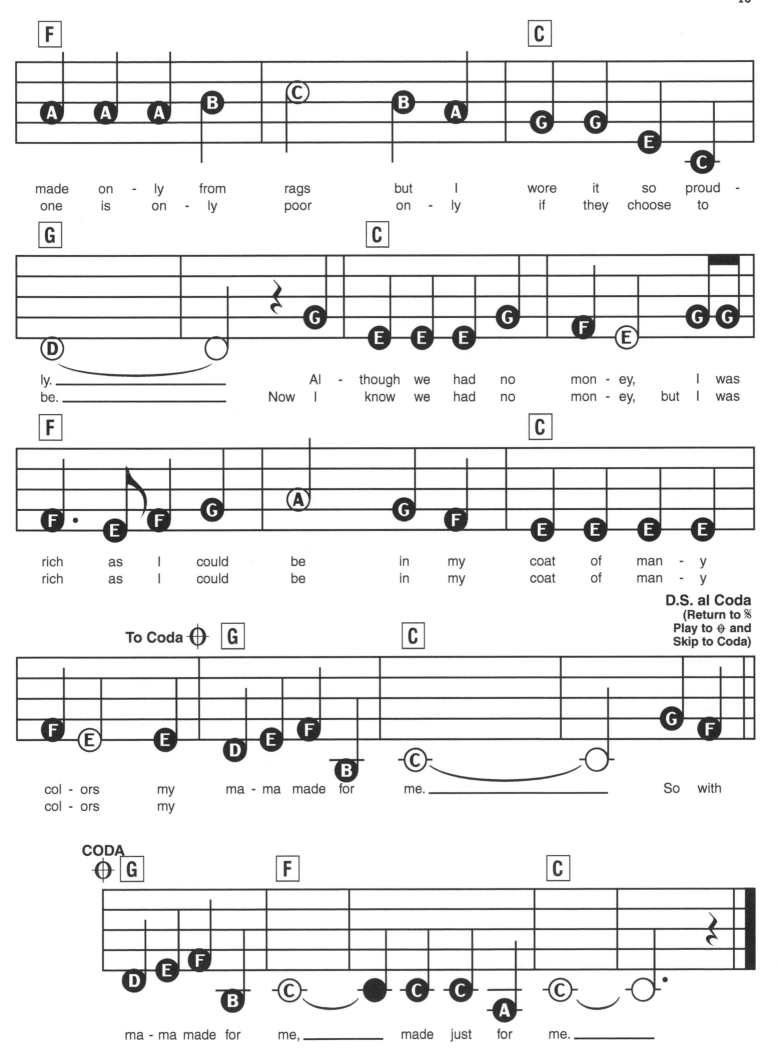

Here You Come Again

Registration 4
Rhythm: Rock or Jazz Rock

Words by Cynthia Weil
Music by Barry Mann

Here you come a - gain,
Here you come a - gain,

just when I've be - gun to get my - self to - geth - er, you
just when I'm a - bout to make it work with - out you, you

waltz right in the door, just like you've done be - fore and
look in - to my eyes just and lie those pret - ty lies and

1

wrap _____ my heart 'round your lit - tle fin - ger.

2

pret - ty soon I'm wond - 'rin' how I came to doubt you.

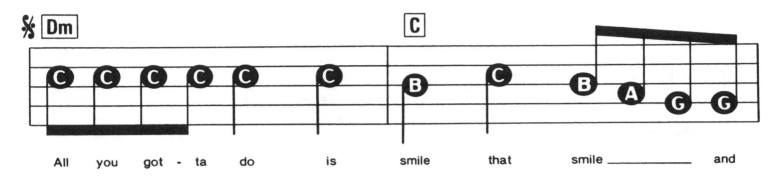

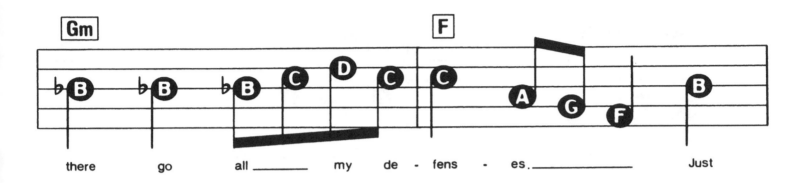

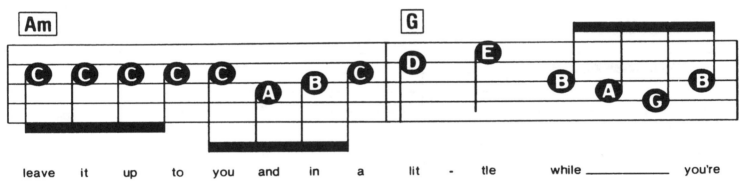

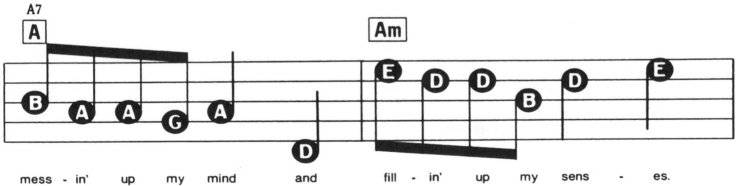

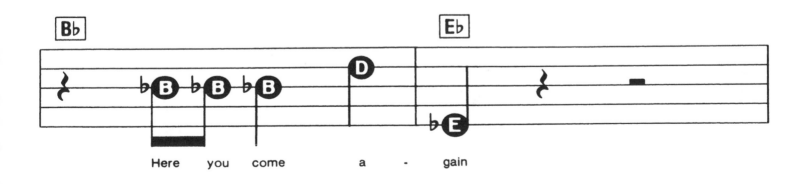

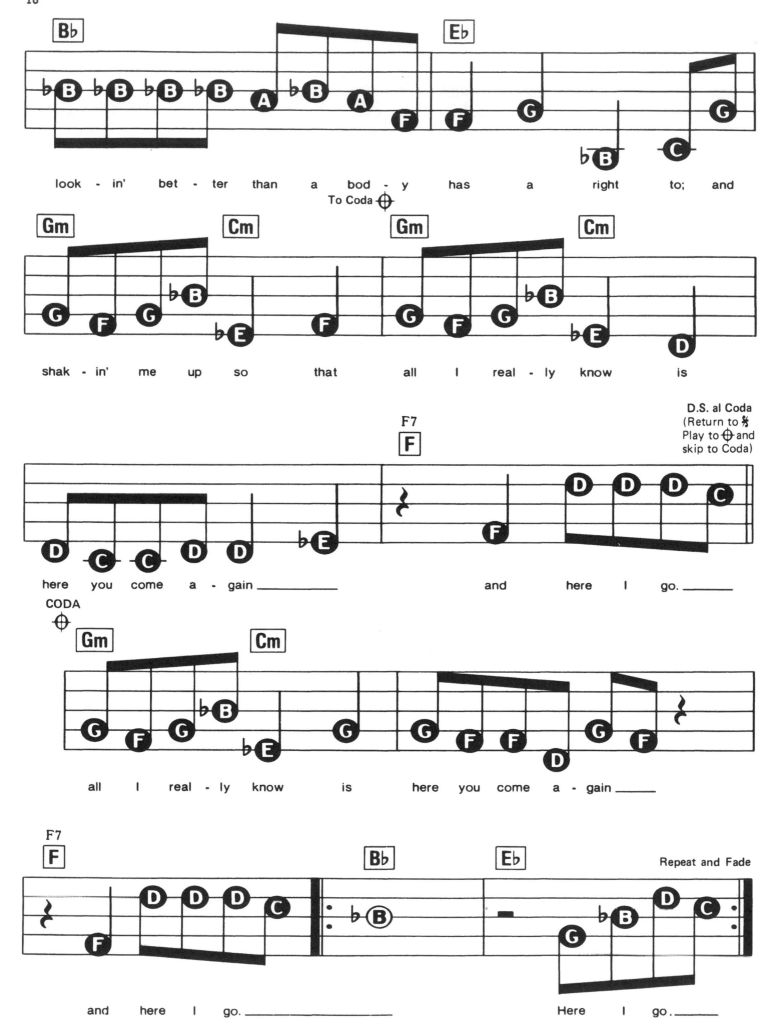

It's All Wrong, But It's All Right

Registration 8
Rhythm: Country Pop or 8 Beat

Words and Music by
Dolly Parton

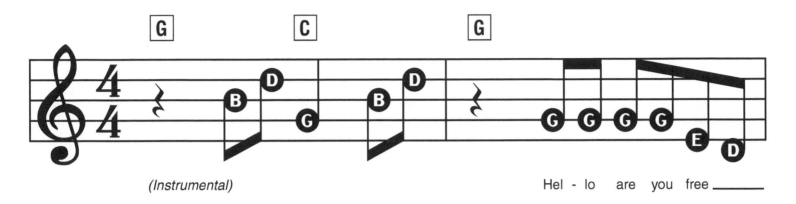

(Instrumental)   Hel - lo are you free _____

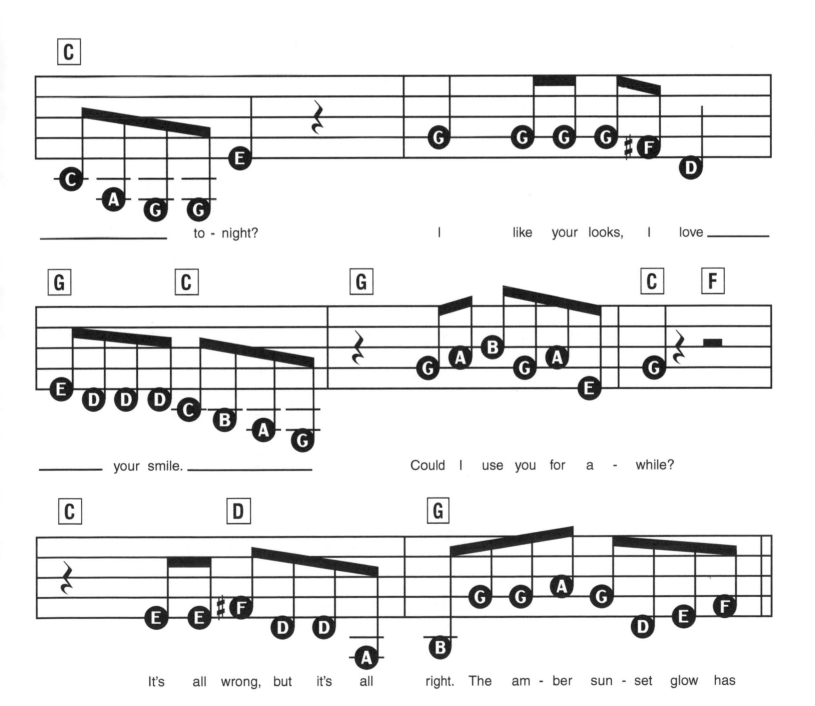

_____   to - night?   I   like your looks, I love _____

_____ your smile. _____   Could I use you for a - while?

It's all wrong, but it's all   right. The am - ber sun - set glow has

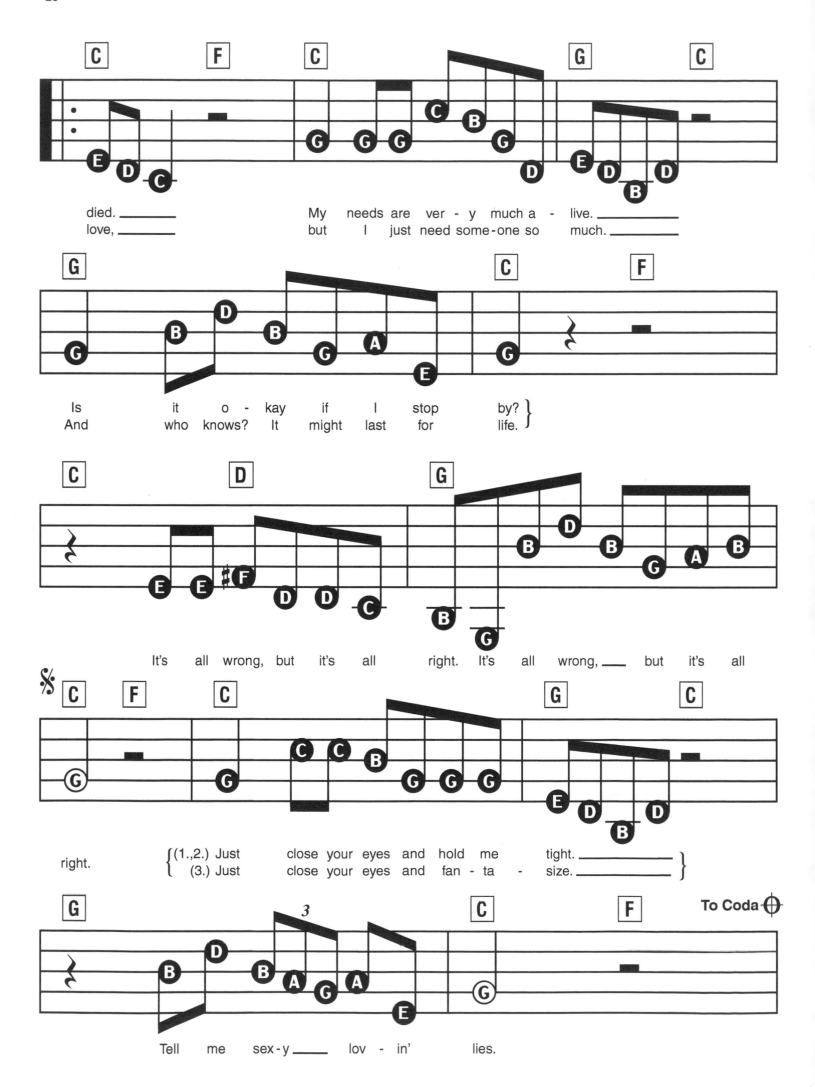

died. _____

love, _____

My needs are ver - y much a - live. _____

but I just need some-one so much. _____

Is it o - kay if I stop by? }

And who knows? It might last for life. }

It's all wrong, but it's all right. It's all wrong, ___ but it's all

right. {(1.,2.) Just close your eyes and hold me tight. _____ }

{(3.) Just close your eyes and fan - ta - size. _____ }

To Coda

Tell me sex - y _____ lov - in' lies.

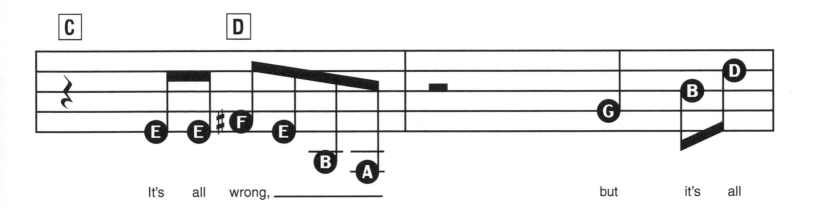

It's all wrong, _____ but it's all

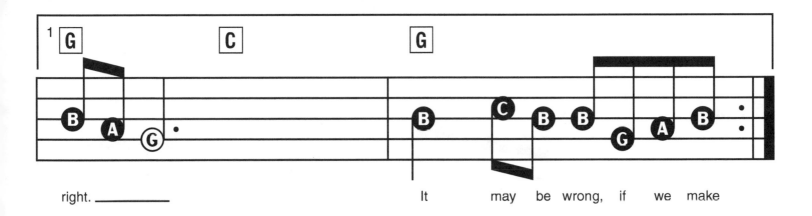

right. _____ It may be wrong, if we make

D.S. al Coda
(Return to %
Play to ⊕ and
Skip to Coda)

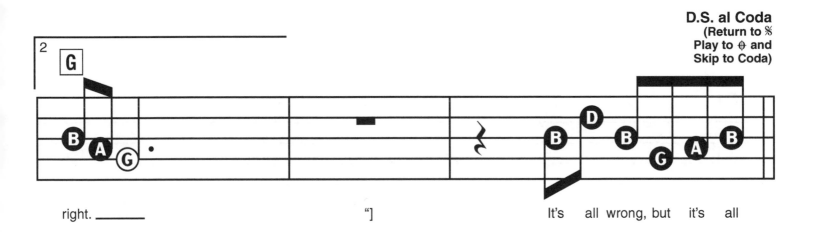

right. _____ "] It's all wrong, but it's all

CODA

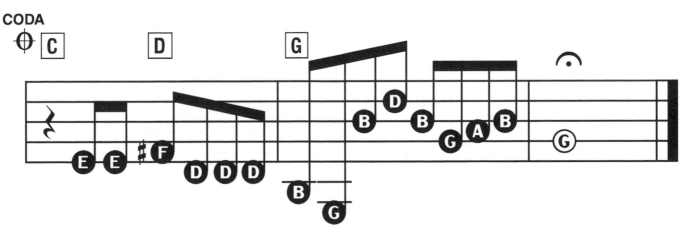

It's all wrong, but it's all right. It's all wrong, _ but it's all right.

I Will Always Love You

Registration 3
Rhythm: Pops or 8 Beat

Words and Music by
Dolly Parton

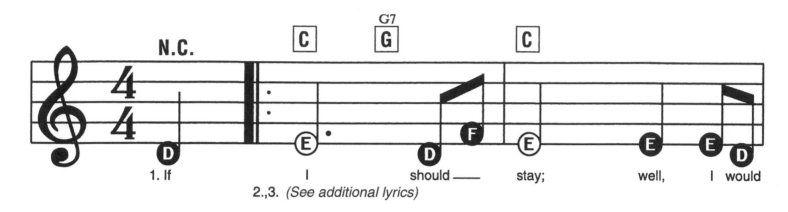

1. If I should —— stay; well, I would

2.,3. *(See additional lyrics)*

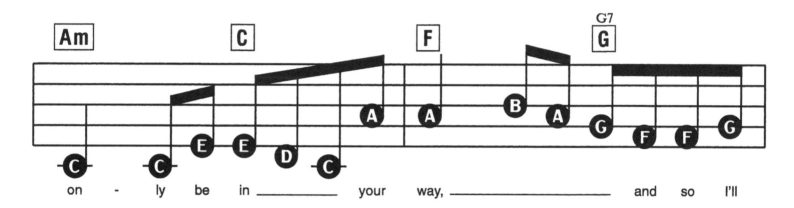

on - ly be in _____ your way, _____ and so I'll

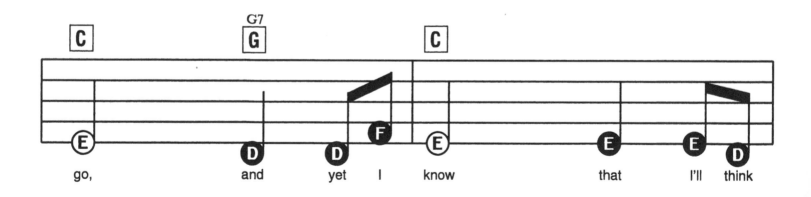

go, and yet I know that I'll think

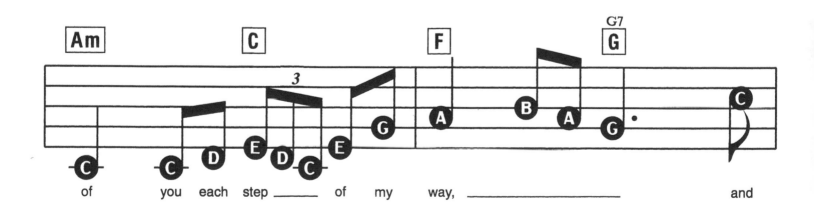

of you each step ___ of my way, _____ and

CHORUS

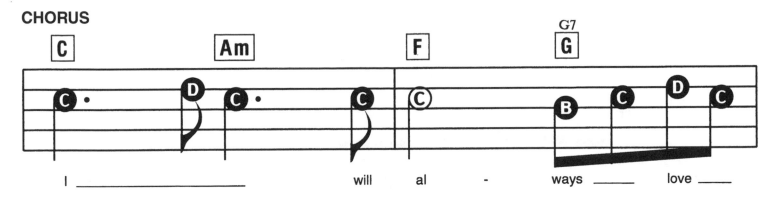

I _____ will al - ways ___ love ___

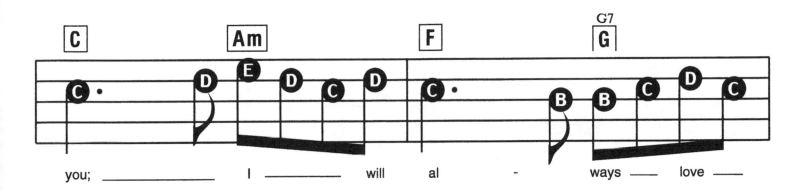

you; _____ I _____ will al - ways ___ love ___

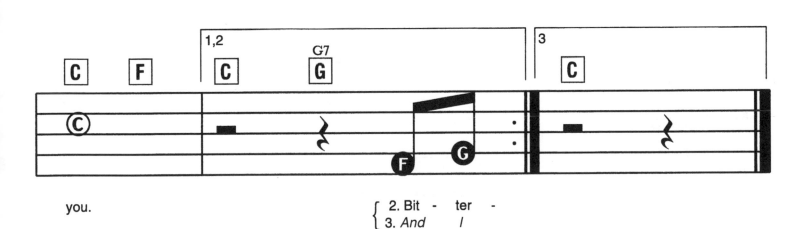

you.

{ 2. Bit - ter -
{ 3. *And   I*

Additional Lyrics

2. Bittersweet memories, that's all I have and all I'm taking with me.
   Good-bye, oh please don't cry, 'cause we both know that I'm not what you need. But…
   Chorus

   (Spoken:)
3. *And I hope life will treat you kind, and I hope that you have all that you ever dreamed of.*
   Oh, I do wish you joy, and I wish you happiness, but above all this, I wish you love. And…
   Chorus

Islands in the Stream

Registration 3
Rhythm: Rock

Words and Music by Barry Gibb,
Robin Gibb and Maurice Gibb

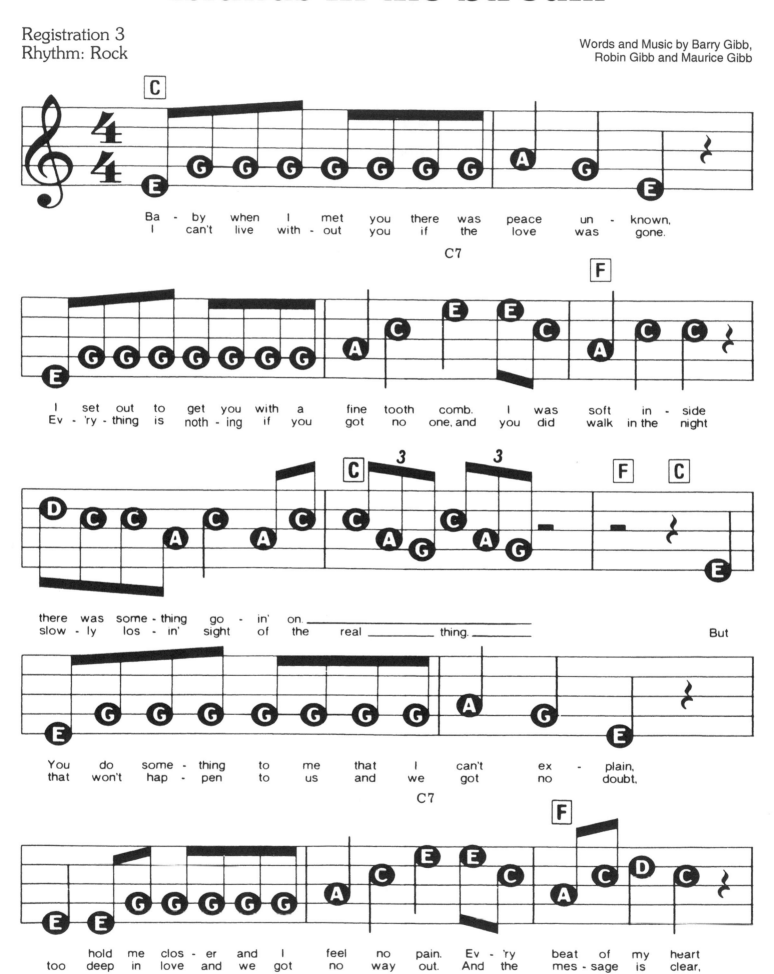

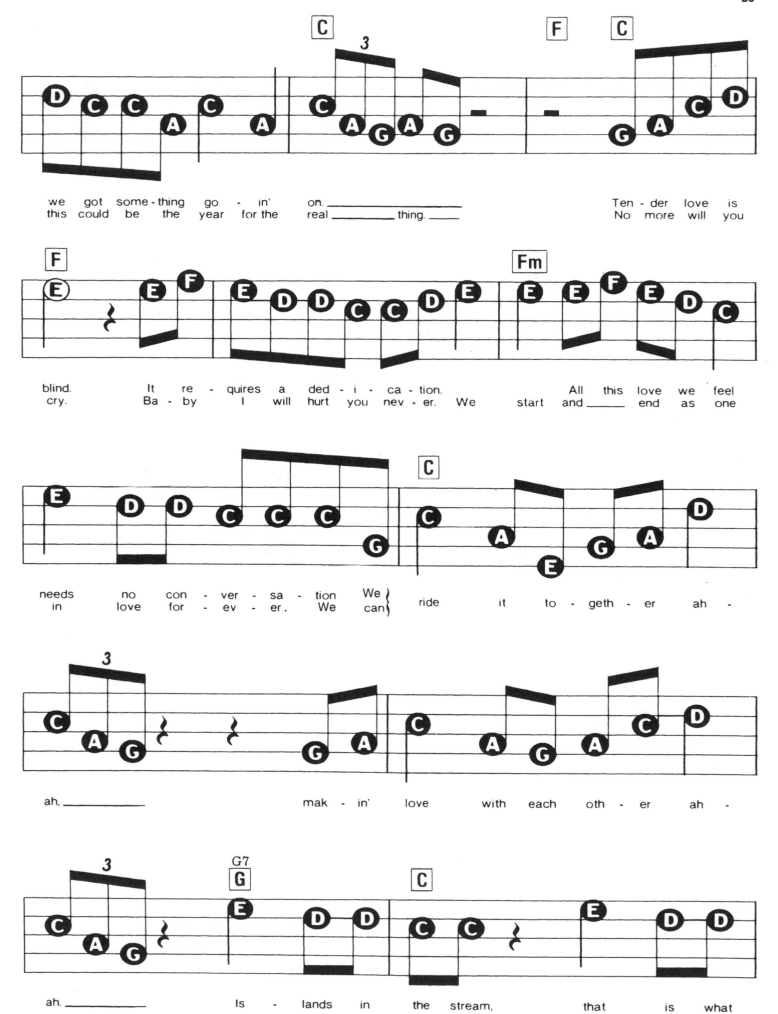

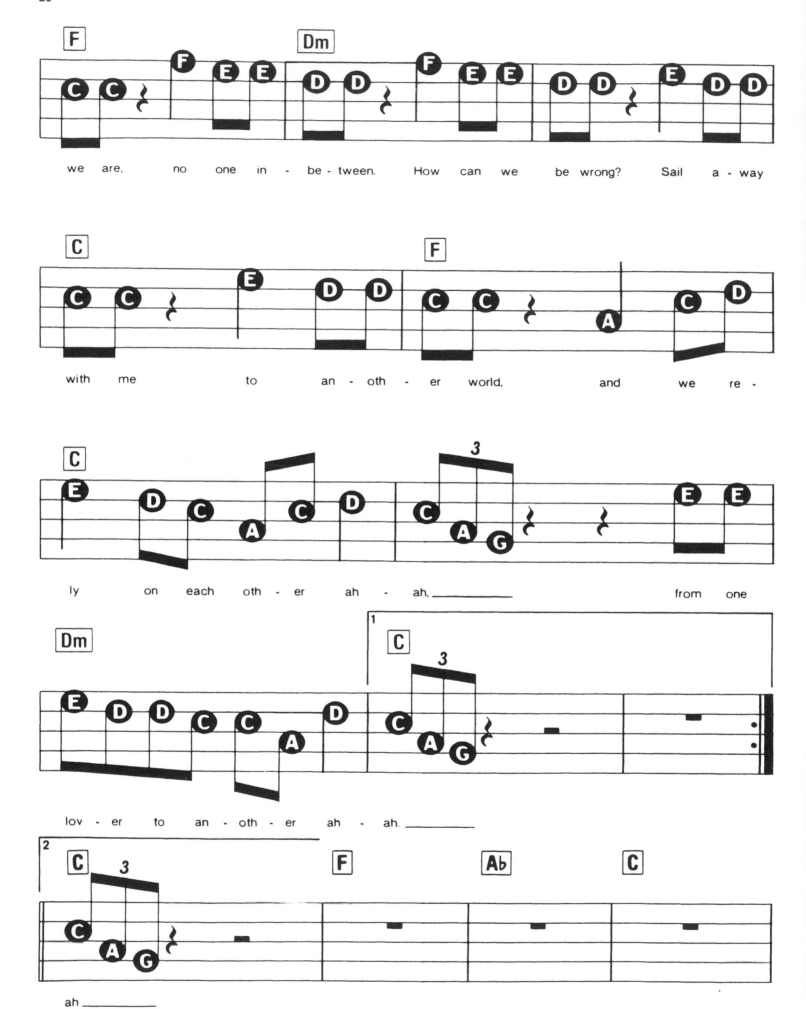

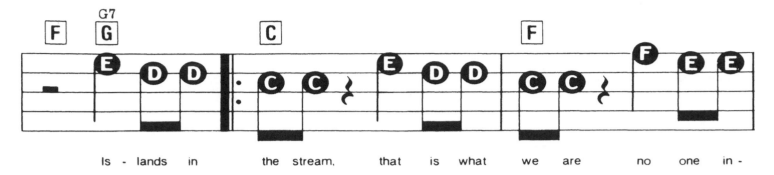

Is - lands in   the stream,   that   is   what   we   are   no   one   in -

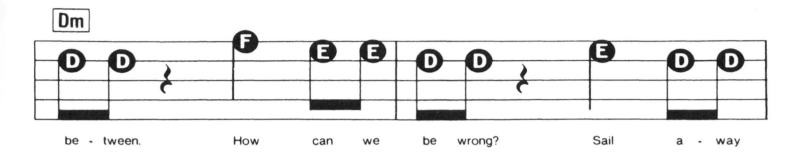

be - tween.   How   can   we   be   wrong?   Sail   a - way

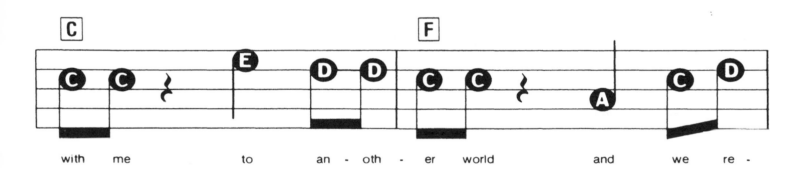

with   me   to   an - oth - er   world   and   we   re -

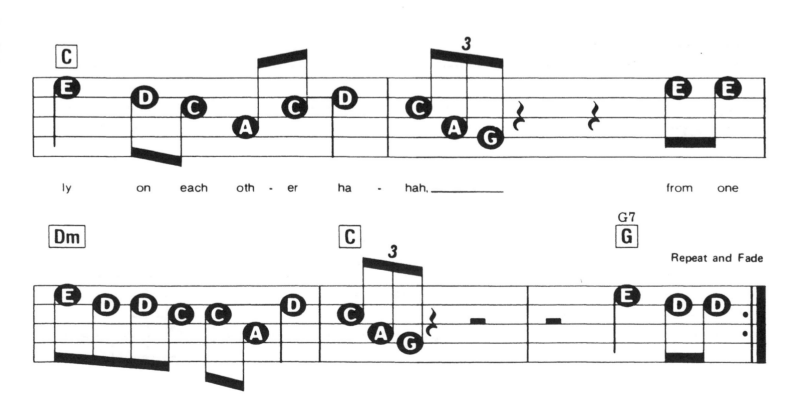

ly   on   each   oth - er   ha - hah, _____   from   one

lov - er   to   an - oth - er   ha - hah. _____   Is - lands in

Jolene

Registration 7
Rhythm: Country Pop or 8 Beat

Words and Music by
Dolly Parton

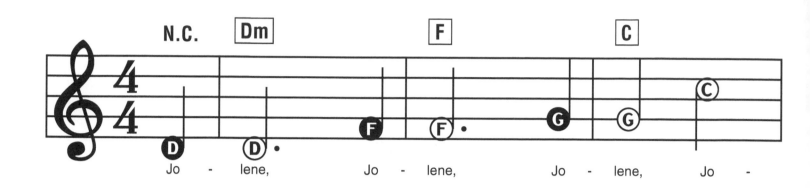

Jo - lene,   Jo - lene,   Jo - lene,   Jo -

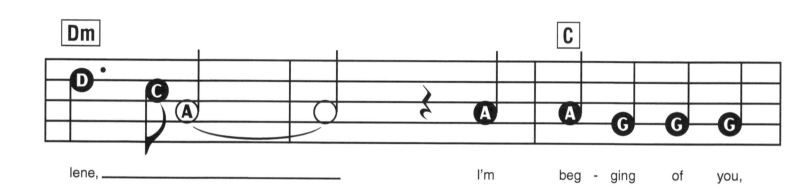

lene, _____   I'm   beg - ging   of   you,

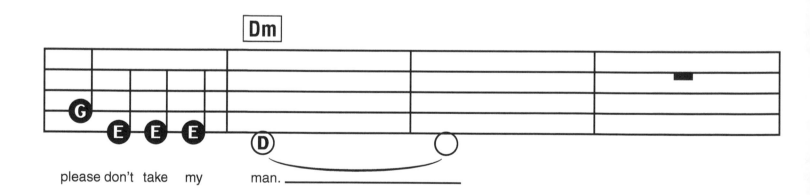

please don't take   my   man. _____

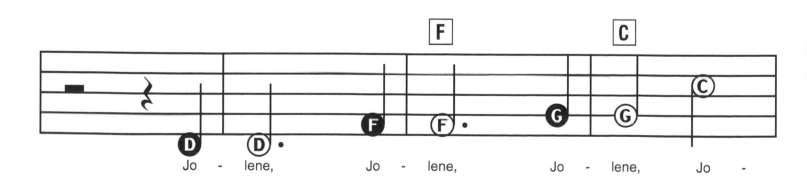

Jo - lene,   Jo - lene,   Jo - lene,   Jo -

29

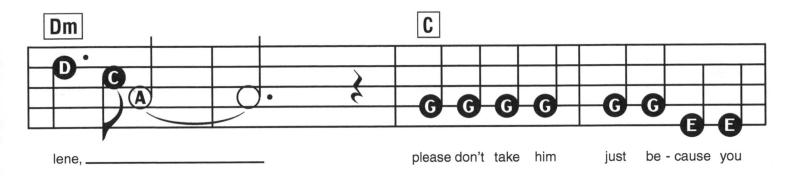

lene, _____ please don't take him just be - cause you

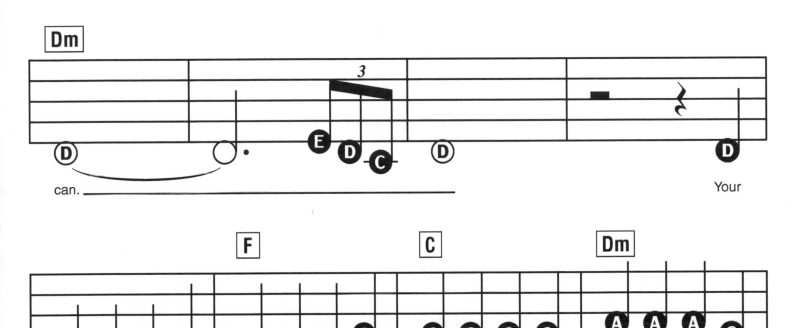

can. _____ Your

beau - ty is be - yond com - pare, with flam - ing locks of au - burn hair, with

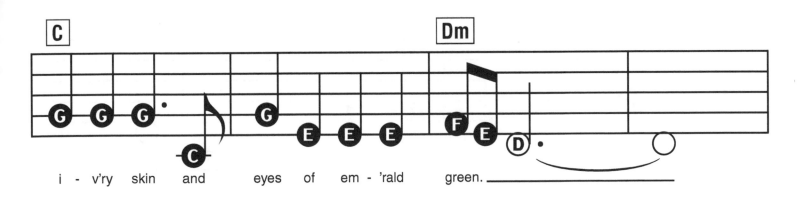

i - v'ry skin and eyes of em - 'rald green. _____

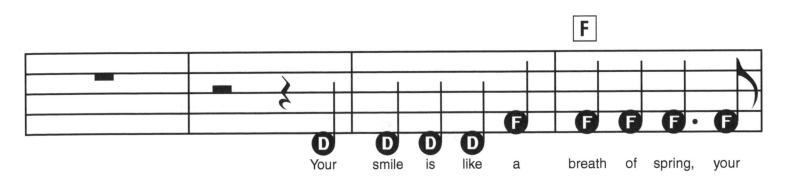

Your smile is like a breath of spring, your

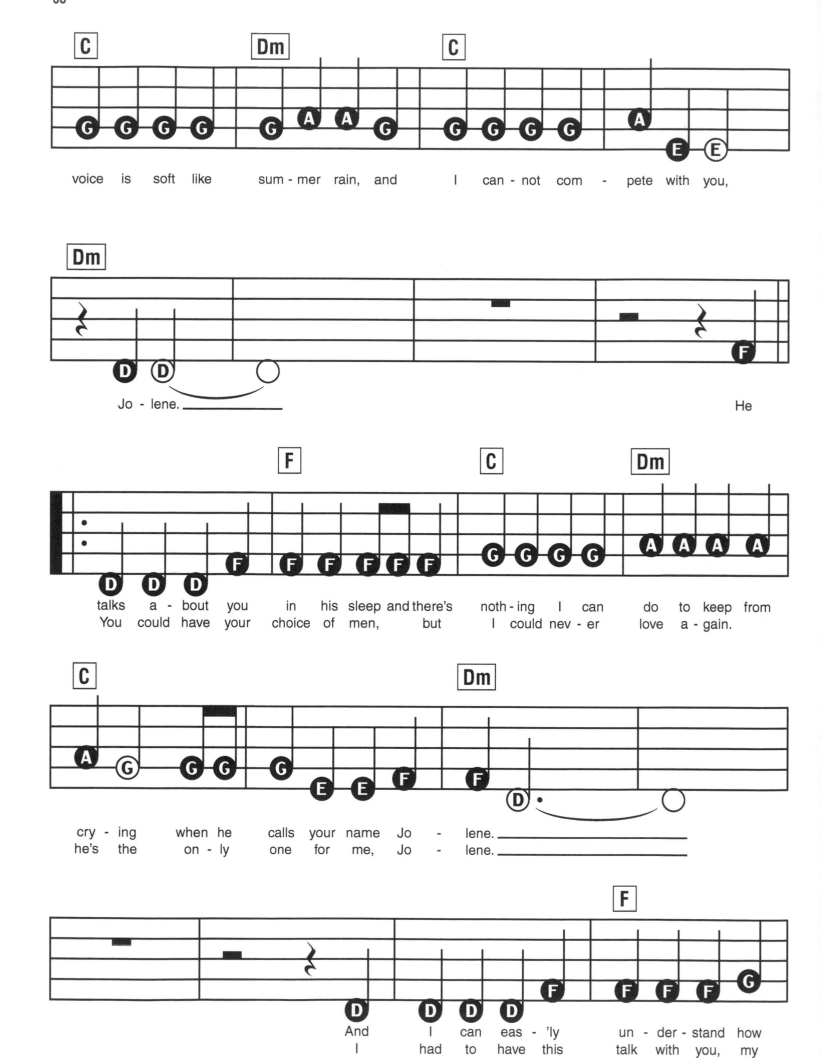

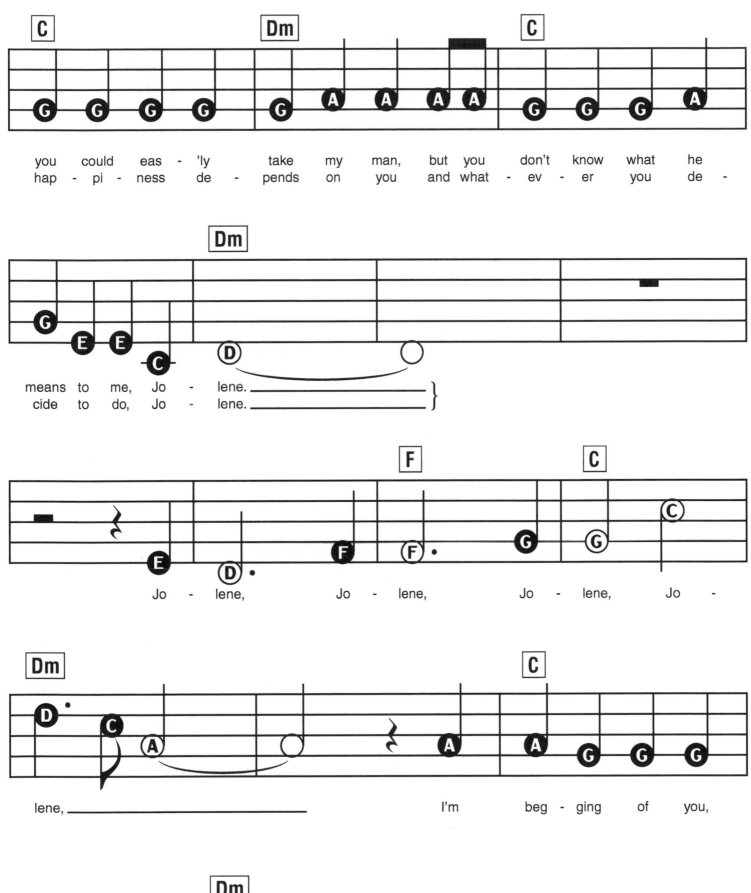

you could eas - 'ly take my man, but you don't know what he
hap - pi - ness de - pends on you and what - ev - er you de -

means to me, Jo - lene. _____ }
cide to do, Jo - lene. _____ }

Jo - lene, Jo - lene, Jo - lene, Jo -

lene, _____ I'm beg - ging of you,

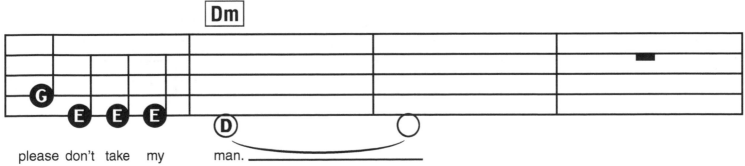

please don't take my man. _____

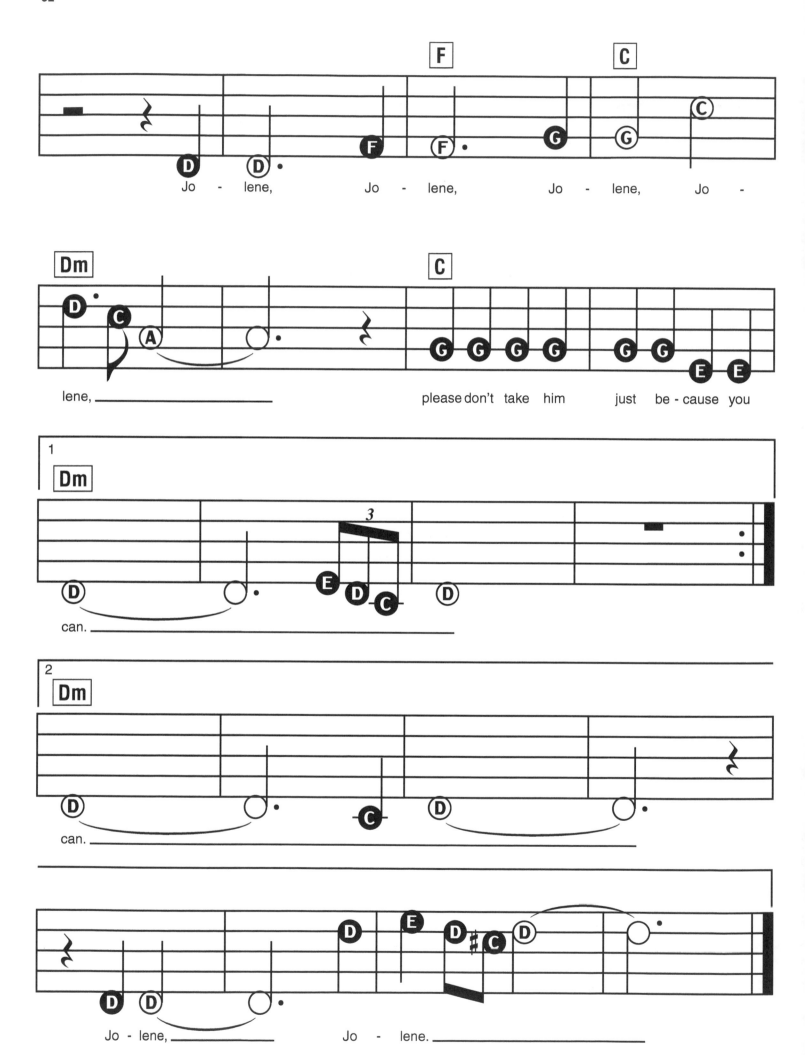

Joshua

Registration 2
Rhythm: Country Swing or Fox Trot

Words and Music by
Dolly Parton

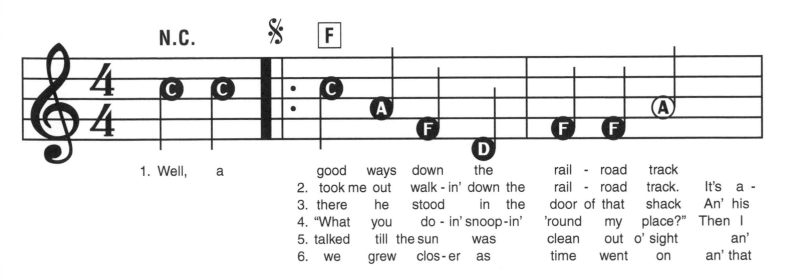

1. Well, a   good   ways   down   the   rail - road   track
2. took me out   walk - in' down the   rail - road   track.   It's a -
3. there   he   stood   in   the   door of that shack   An' his
4. "What   you   do - in' snoop-in'   'round   my   place?"   Then I
5. talked   till the sun   was   clean   out o' sight   an'
6. we   grew   clos - er   as   time   went   on   an' that

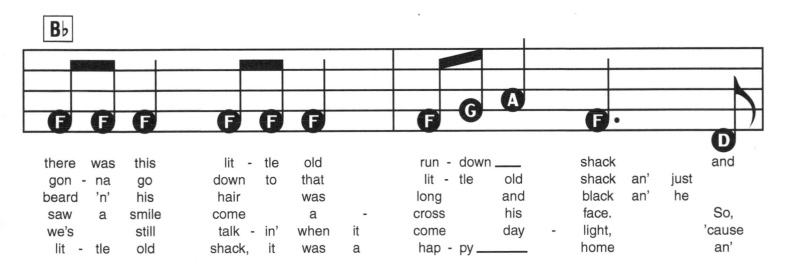

there   was   this   lit - tle   old   run - down _____   shack   and
gon - na   go   down   to   that   lit - tle   old   shack   an'   just
beard 'n'   his   hair   was   long   and   black   an'   he
saw   a   smile   come   a -   cross   his   face.   So,
we's   still   talk - in' when   it   come   day - light,   'cause
lit - tle old   shack,   it   was   a   hap - py _____   home   an'

C7

in   it   lived   a   man   I'd   nev - er   was
find   out   if   all   them things   I'd   heard   was
was   the   big -   gest man   I'd   ev - er   er
I   smiled back   an'   I   told   him   who   I
there was   just   so   much   we   had   to
we   just could - n't   help   but   fall   in

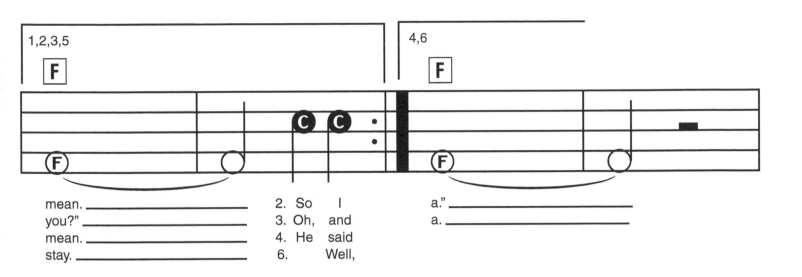

mean. _____
you?" _____
mean. _____
stay. _____

2. So I
3. Oh, and
4. He said
6. Well,

a." _____
a. _____

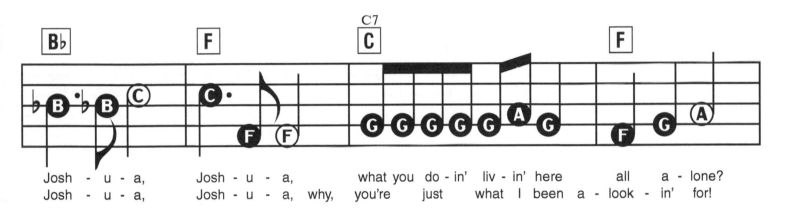

Josh - u - a, Josh - u - a, what you do-in' liv-in' here all a - lone?
Josh - u - a, Josh - u - a, why, you're just what I been a - look - in' for!

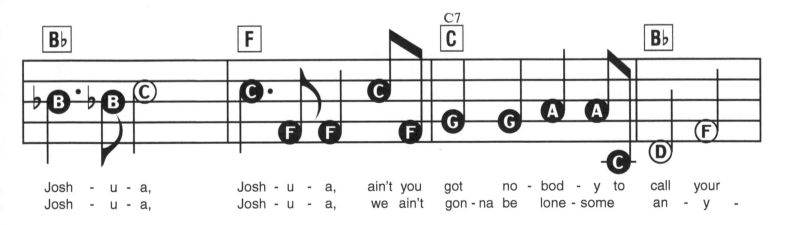

Josh - u - a, Josh - u - a, ain't you got no - bod - y to call your
Josh - u - a, Josh - u - a, we ain't gon - na be lone - some an - y -

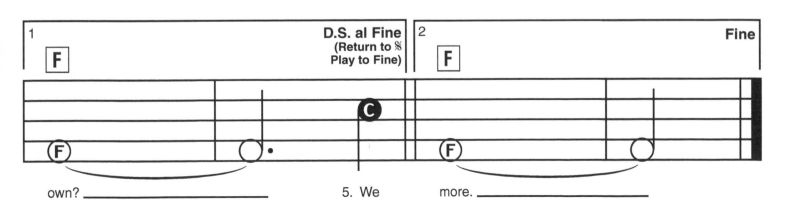

D.S. al Fine
(Return to %
Play to Fine)

Fine

own? _____

5. We

more. _____

Love Is Like a Butterfly

Registration 2
Rhythm: Country Swing or Fox Trot

Words and Music by
Dolly Parton

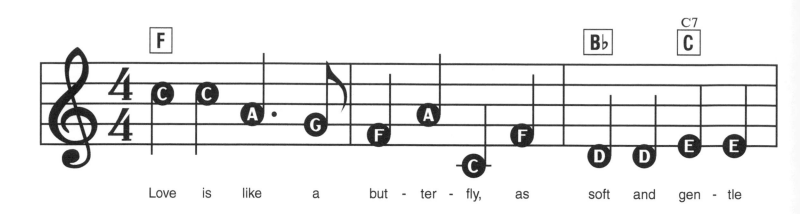

Love   is   like   a   but - ter - fly,   as   soft   and   gen - tle

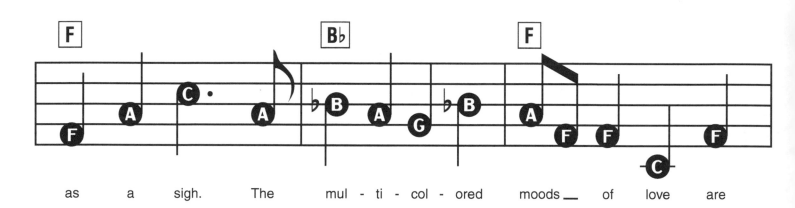

as   a   sigh.   The   mul - ti - col - ored   moods ___   of   love   are

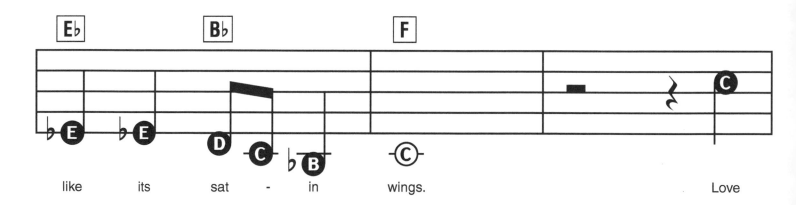

like   its   sat - in   wings.   Love

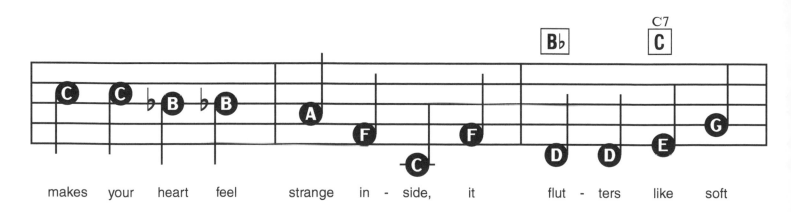

makes   your   heart   feel   strange   in - side,   it   flut - ters   like   soft

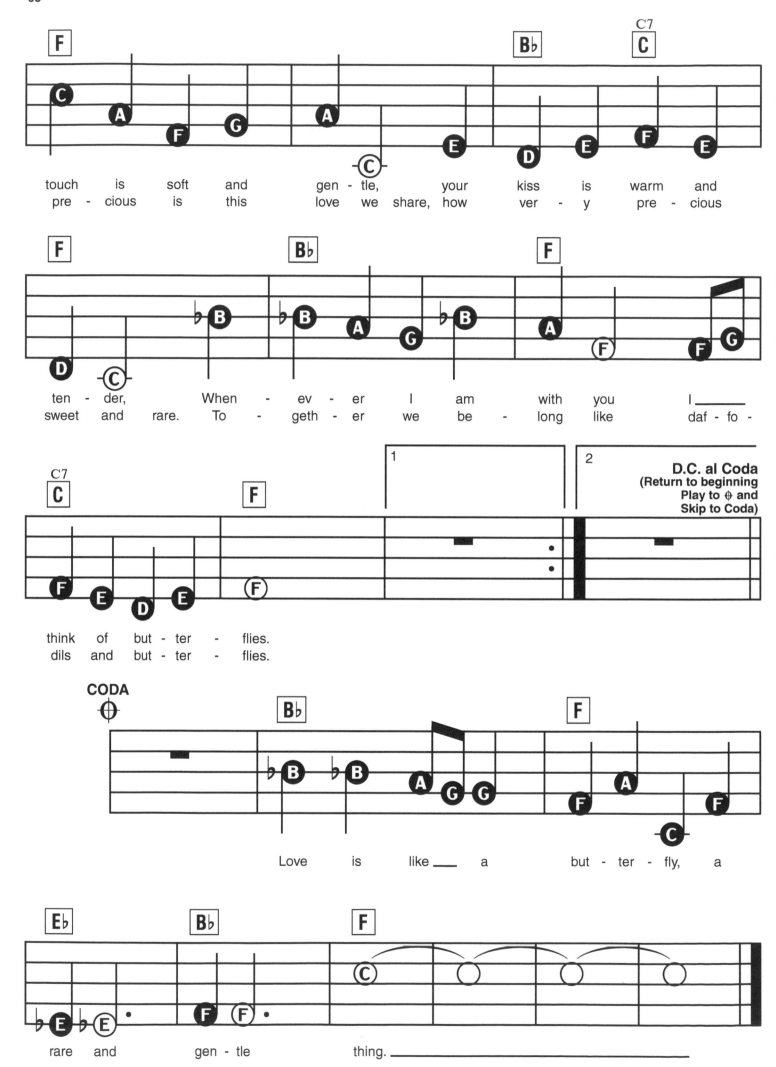

Nine to Five
from NINE TO FIVE

Registration 5
Rhythm: Rock

Words and Music by
Dolly Parton

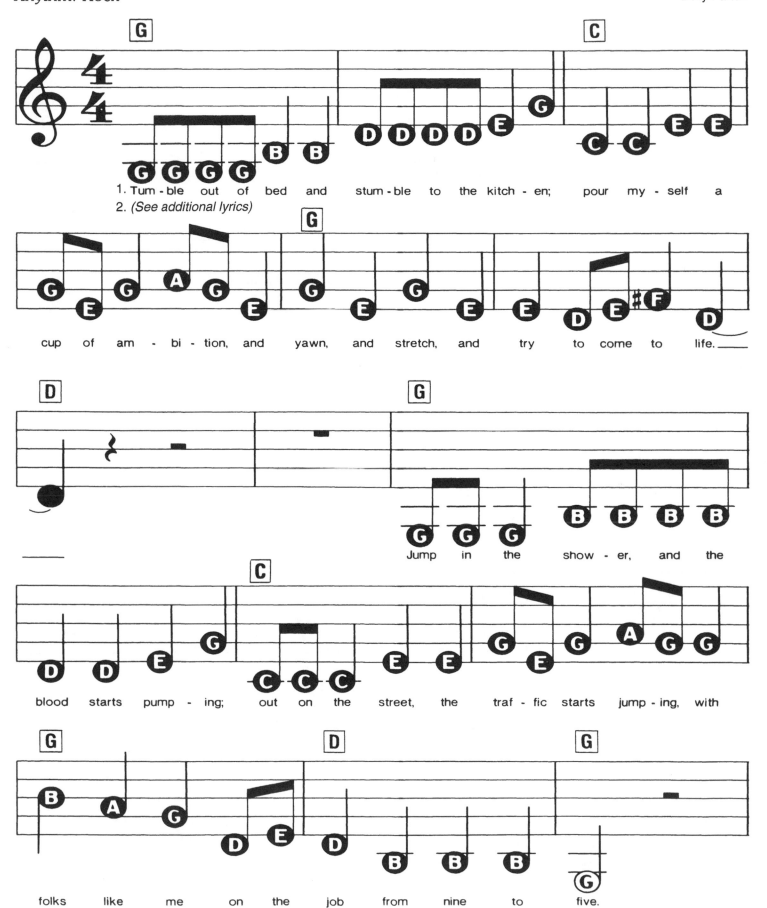

1. Tum-ble out of bed and stum-ble to the kitch-en; pour my-self a
2. *(See additional lyrics)*

cup of am-bi-tion, and yawn, and stretch, and try to come to life. ___

___ Jump in the show-er, and the

blood starts pump-ing; out on the street, the traf-fic starts jump-ing, with

folks like me on the job from nine to five.

CHORUS

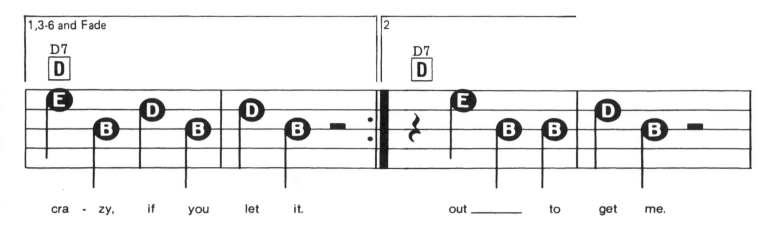

1,3-6 and Fade

cra - zy,   if   you   let   it.

out _____ to   get   me.

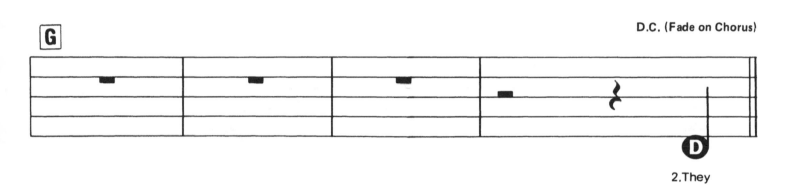

D.C. (Fade on Chorus)

2.They

Additional Lyrics

Verse 2:
They let you dream just to watch them shatter;
You're just a step on the boss man's ladder,
But you've got dreams he'll never take away.
In the same boat with a lot of your friends;
Waitin' for the day your ship'll come in,
And the tide's gonna turn, and it's all gonna roll your way.
Chorus

Chorus 4,6:
Nine to five, they've got you where they want you;
There's a better life, and you dream about it, don't you?
It's a rich man's game, no matter what they call it;
And you spend your life putting money in his pocket.

Tennessee Homesick Blues

Registration 7
Rhythm: Country Pop or 8 Beat

Words and Music by
Dolly Parton

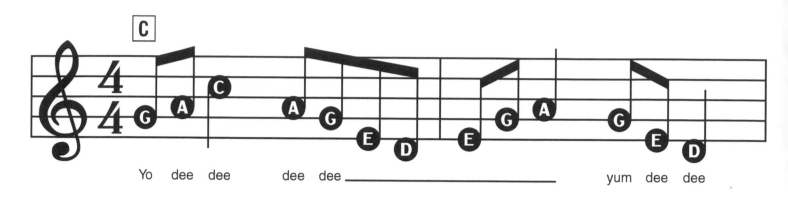

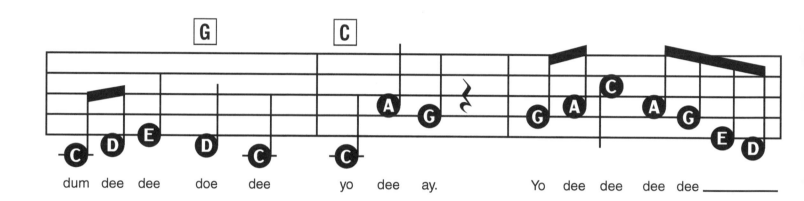

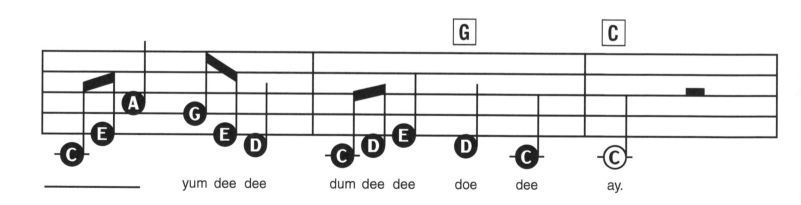

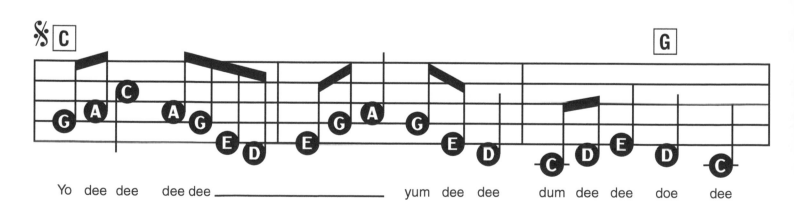

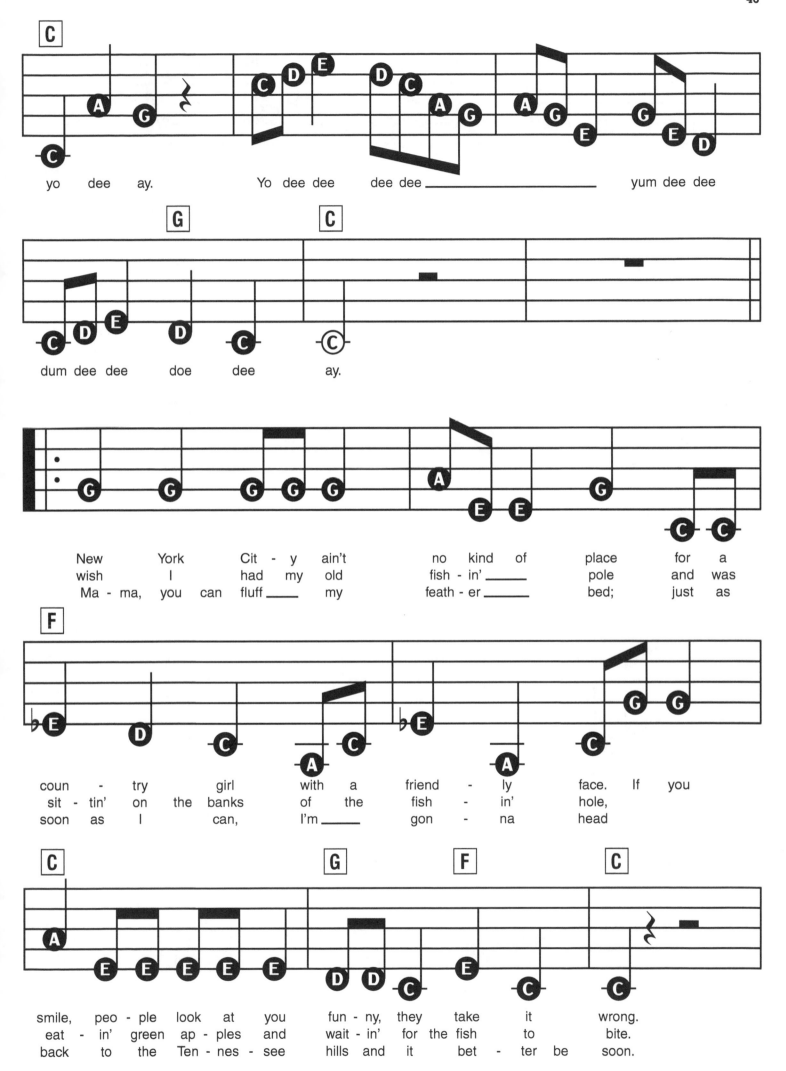

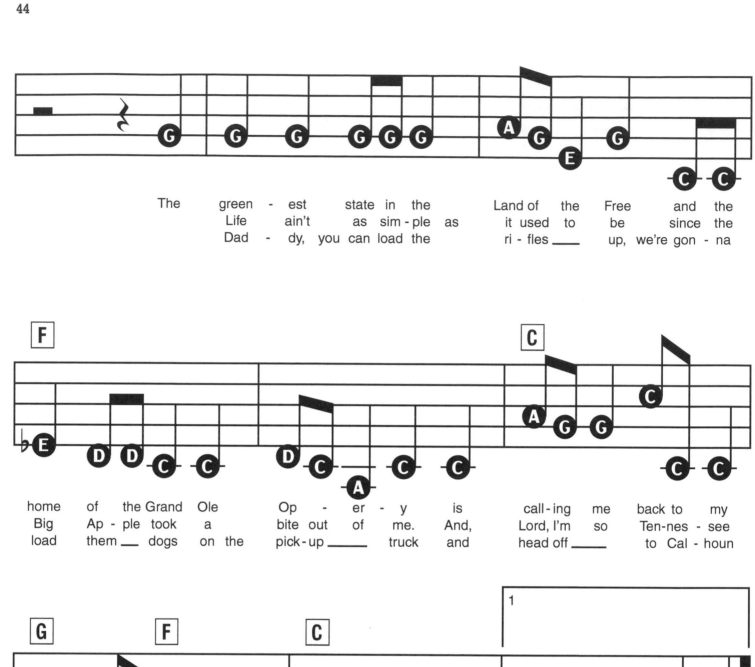

The green-est state in the Land of the Free and the
Life ain't as sim-ple as it used to be since the
Dad - dy, you can load the ri-fles ___ up, we're gon - na

home of the Grand Ole Op - er - y is call-ing me back to my
Big Ap - ple took a bite out of me. And, Lord, I'm so Ten-nes - see
load them ___ dogs on the pick-up ___ truck and head off ___ to Cal - houn

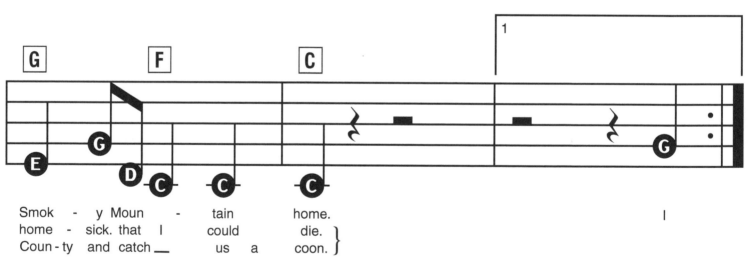

| 1 |

Smok - y Moun - tain home.
home - sick. that I could die.
Coun - ty and catch ___ us a coon. }

| 2,3 |

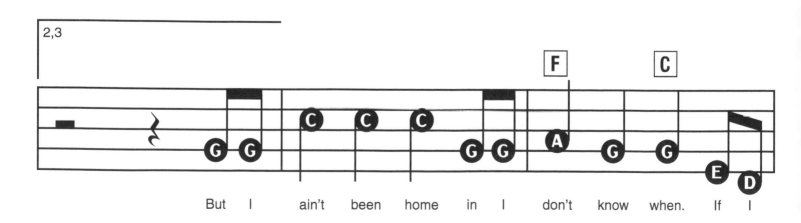

But I ain't been home in I don't know when. If I

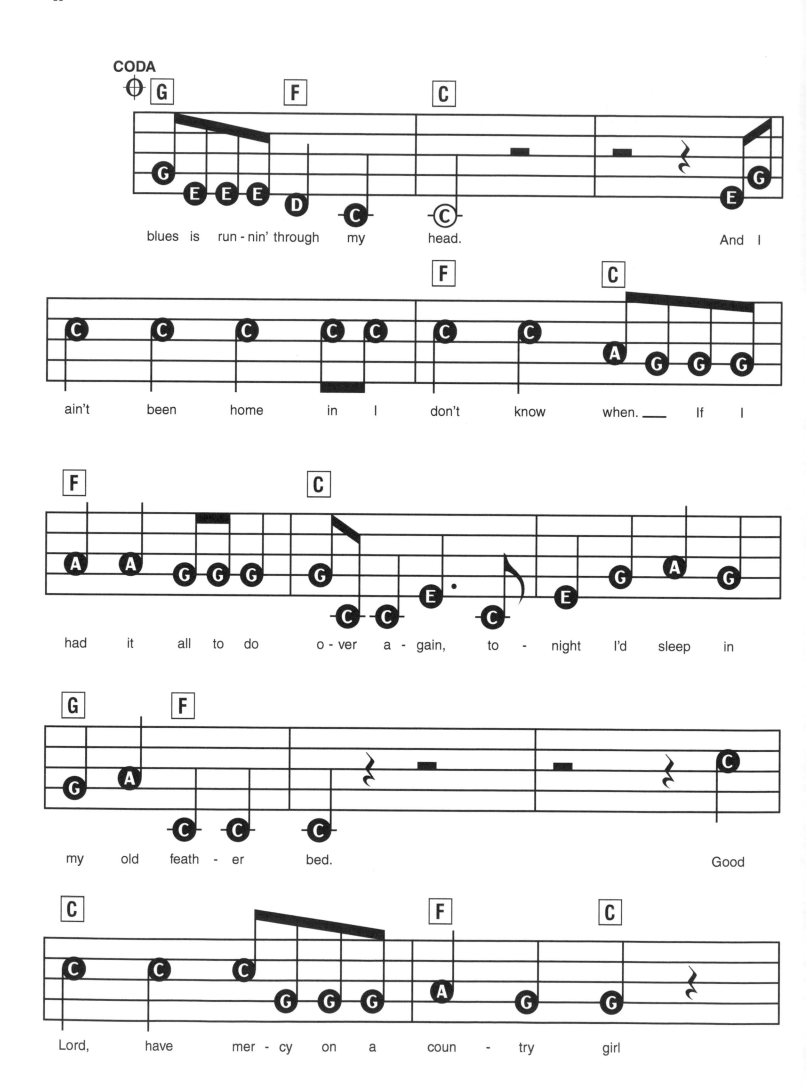

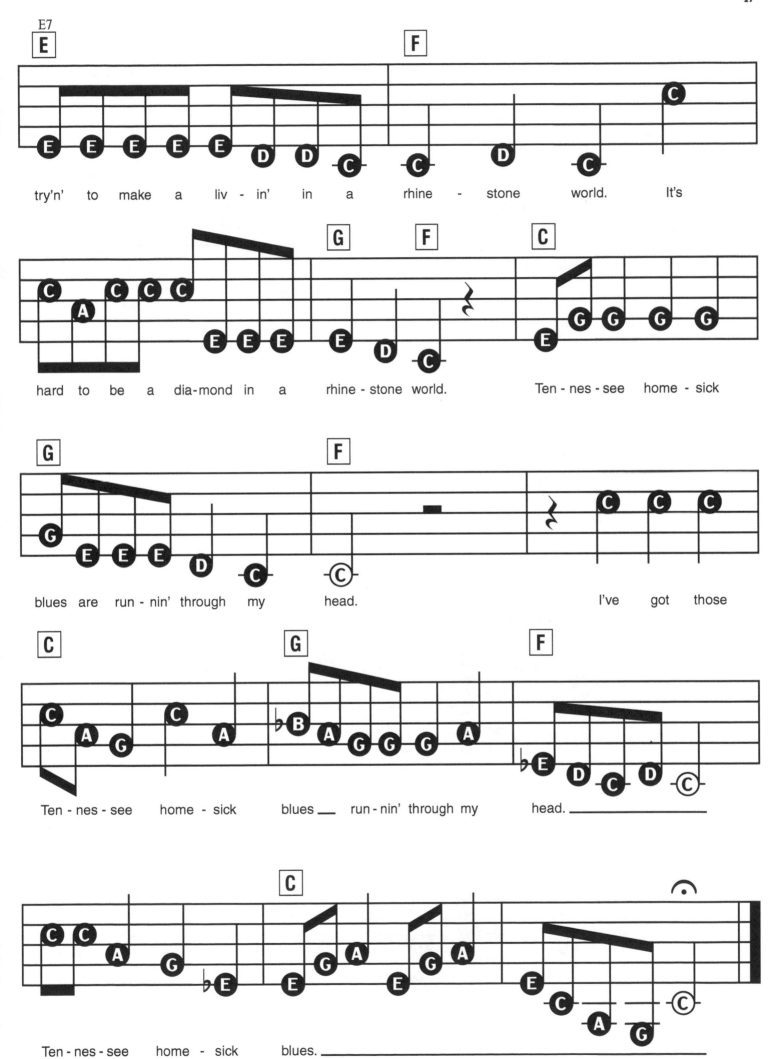

Two Doors Down

Registration 4
Rhythm: Country Pop or 8 Beat

Words and Music by
Dolly Parton

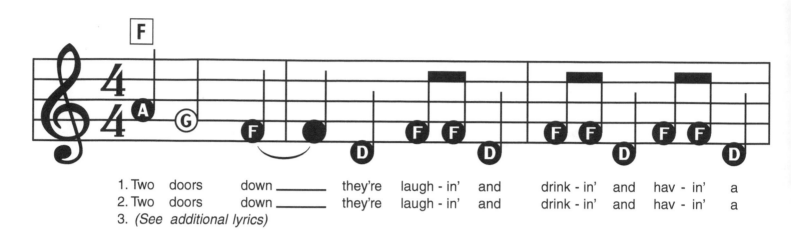

1. Two doors down _____ they're laugh - in' and drink - in' and hav - in' a
2. Two doors down _____ they're laugh - in' and drink - in' and hav - in' a
3. *(See additional lyrics)*

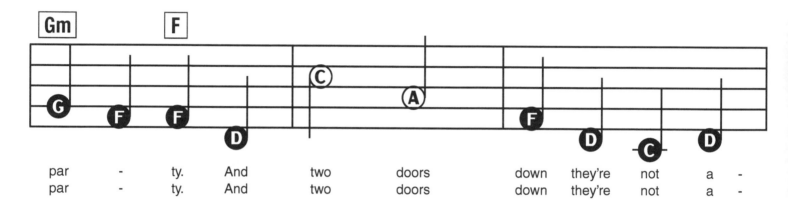

par - ty. And two doors down they're not a -
par - ty. And two doors down they're not a -

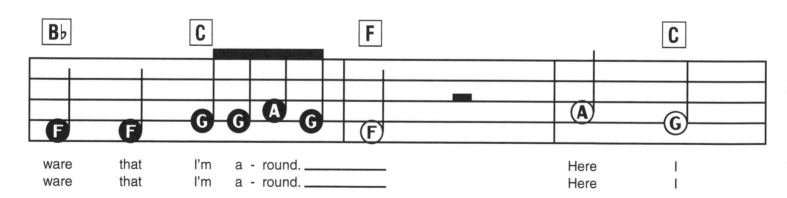

ware that I'm a - round. _____ Here I
ware that I'm a - round. _____ Here I

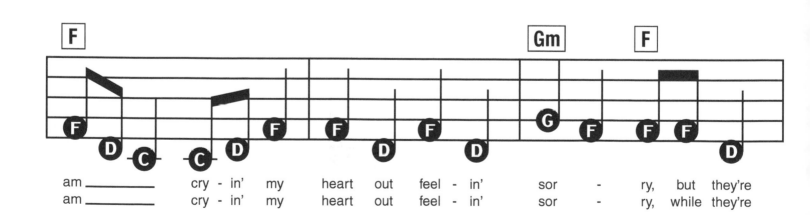

am _____ cry - in' my heart out feel - in' sor - ry, but they're
am _____ cry - in' my heart out feel - in' sor - ry, while they're

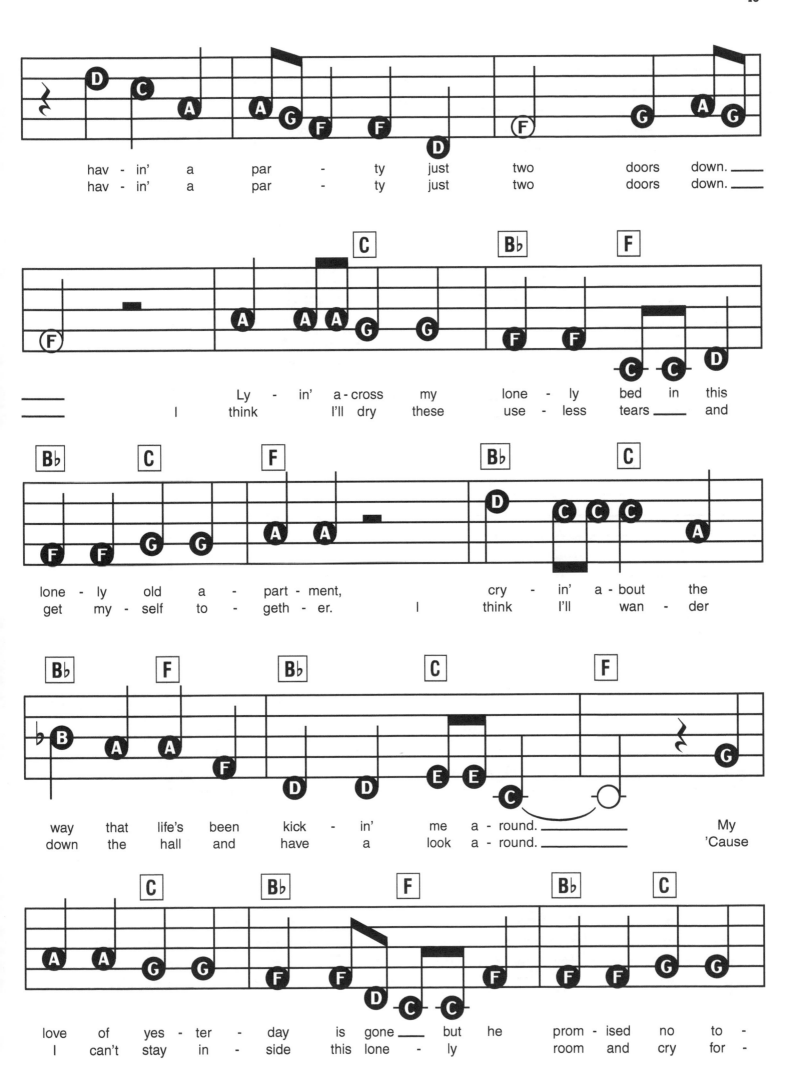

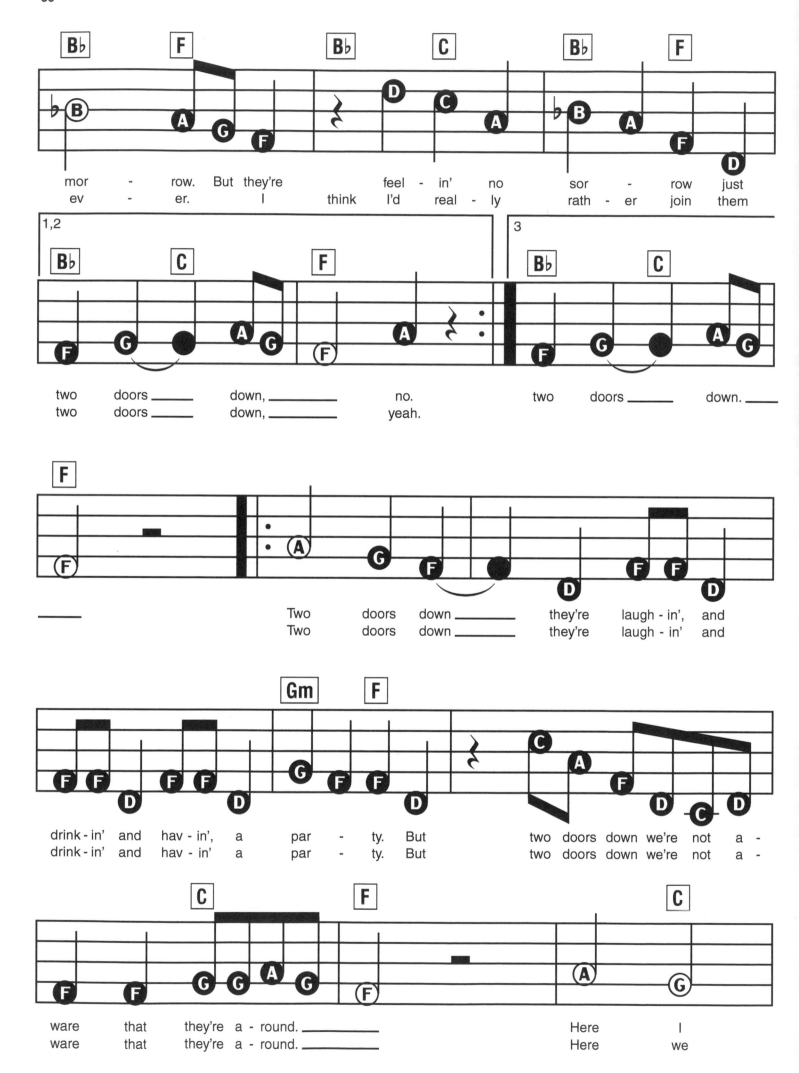

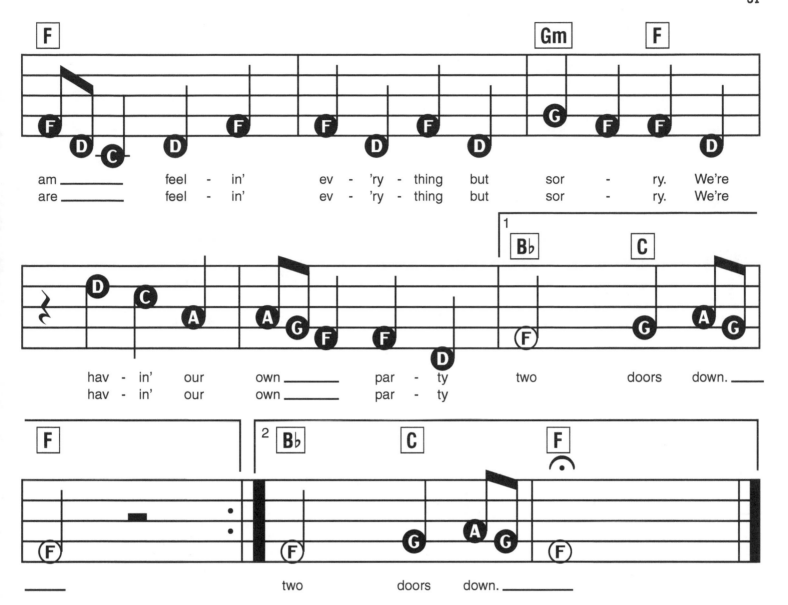

Additional Lyrics

3. Two doors down they're laughin' and drinkin' and havin' a party.
   And two doors down they're all aware that I'm around.
   'Cause here I am no longer cryin', feelin' sorry.
   We're havin' a party just two doors down.

   I can't believe I'm standin' here dry-eyed all smiles and talkin'.
   Makin' conversation with the new love I have found.
   I ask him if he'd like to be alone; so we start walkin'
   Down the hall to my place waitin' two doors down.

Why'd You Come in Here Lookin' Like That

Registration 4
Rhythm: Country Swing or Fox Trot

Words and Music by Randy Thomas
and Bob Carlisle

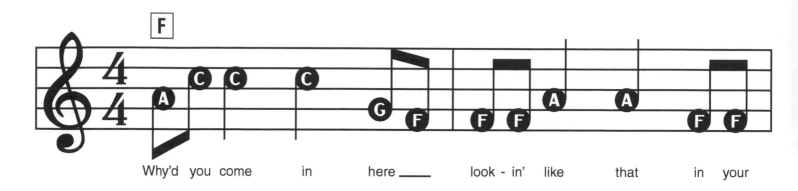

Why'd you come in here ____ look - in' like that in your

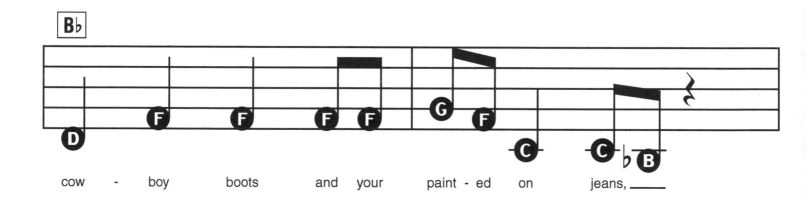

cow - boy boots and your paint - ed on jeans, ____

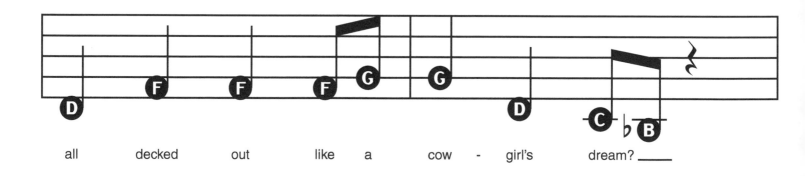

all decked out like a cow - girl's dream? ____

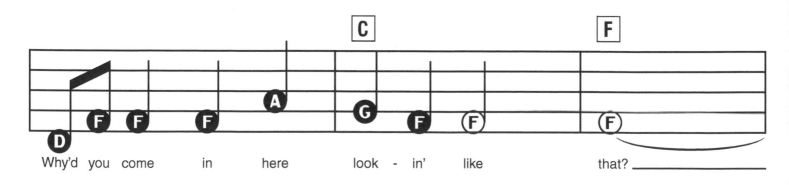

Why'd you come in here look - in' like that? ____

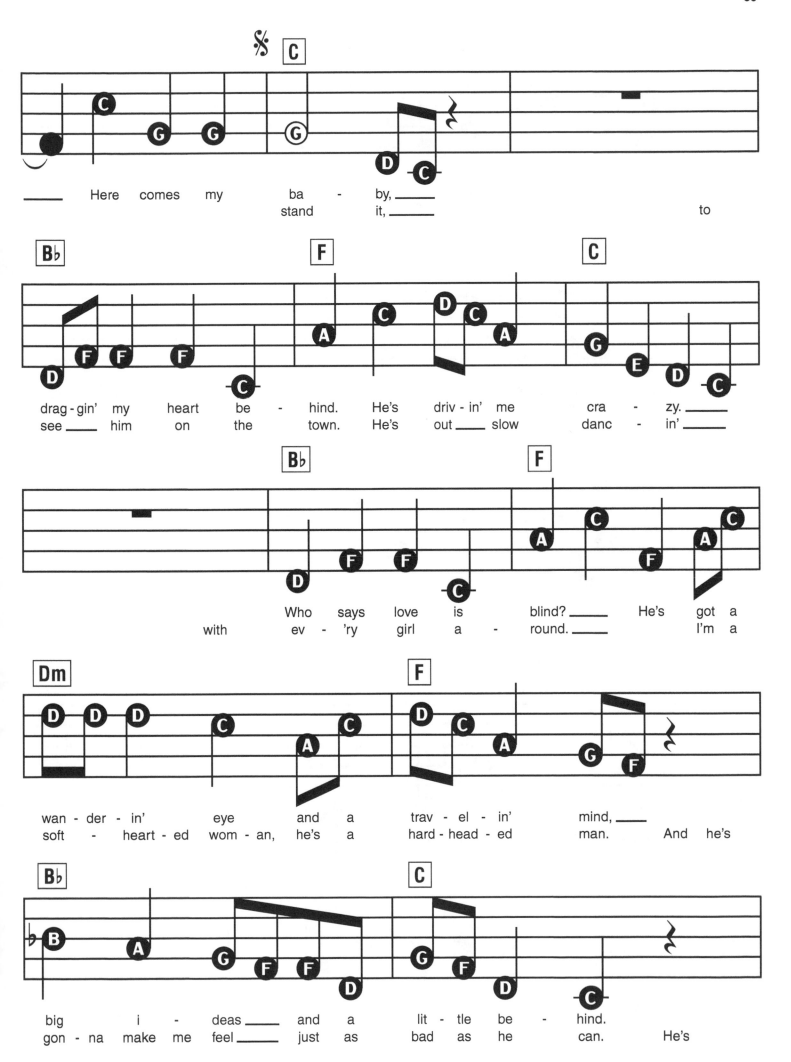

54

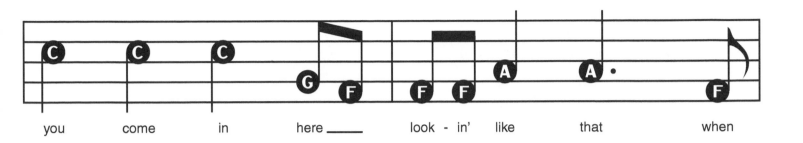

you come in here _____ look - in' like that when

B♭

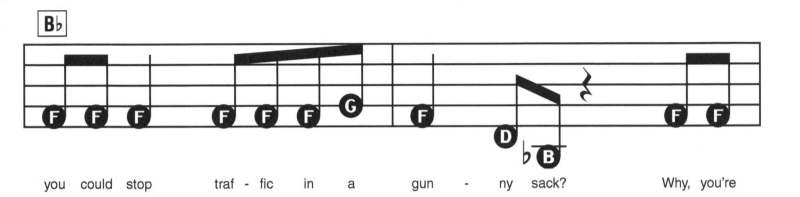

you could stop traf - fic in a gun - ny sack? Why, you're

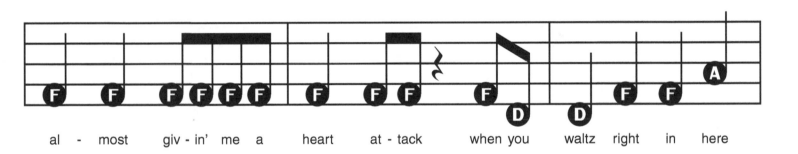

al - most giv - in' me a heart at - tack when you waltz right in here

D.S. al Coda
(Return to 𝄋
Play to ⊕ and
Skip to Coda)

C   **F**

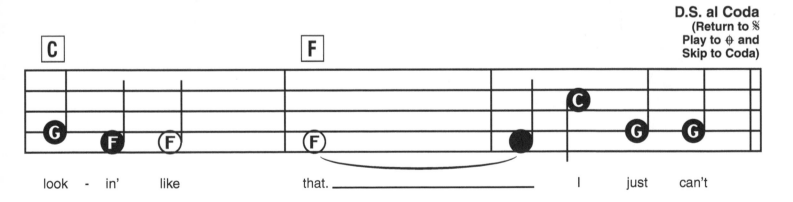

look - in' like that. _____ I just can't

CODA
⊕ **C**   **F**

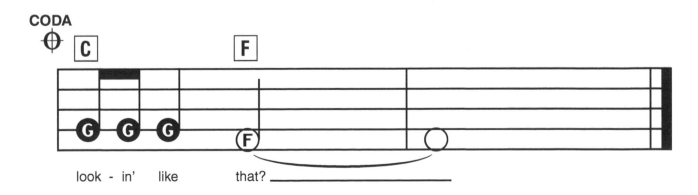

look - in' like that? _____

Yellow Roses

Registration 3
Rhythm: Country Swing or Fox Trot

Words and Music by
Dolly Parton

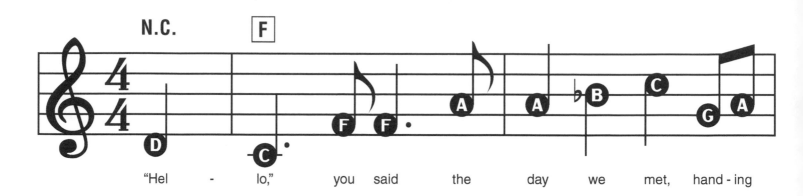

"Hel - lo," you said the day we met, hand - ing

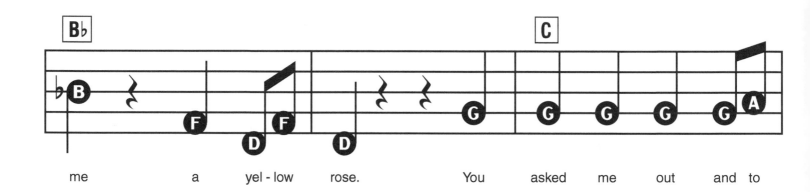

me a yel - low rose. You asked me out and to

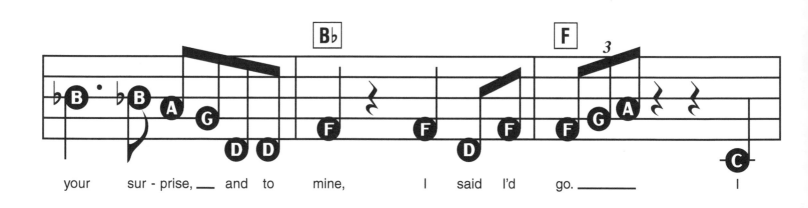

your sur - prise, __ and to mine, I said I'd go. _____ I

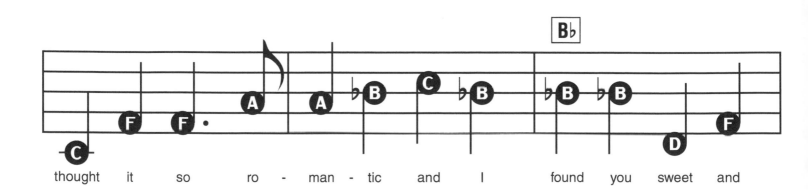

thought it so ro - man - tic and I found you sweet and

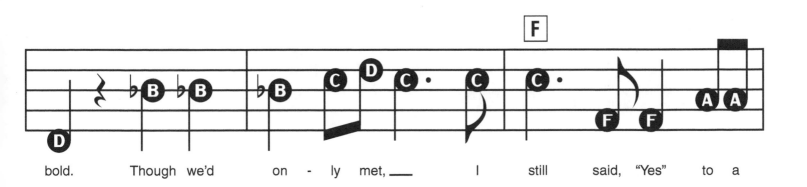

bold.   Though we'd   on - ly met, ___   I   still   said, "Yes"   to a

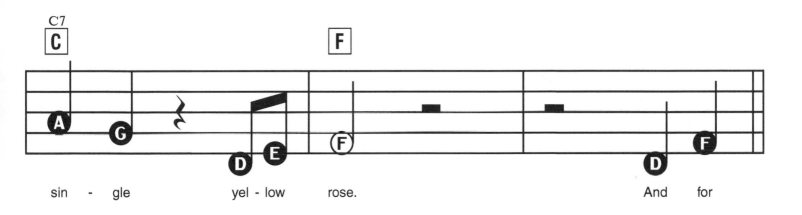

sin - gle   yel - low   rose.   And   for

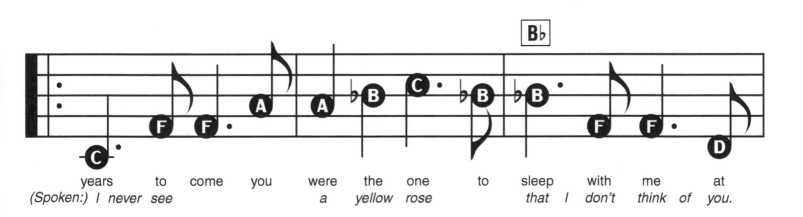

years   to   come   you   were   the   one   to   sleep   with   me   at
(Spoken:) I never see   a   yellow rose   that I   don't   think of   you.

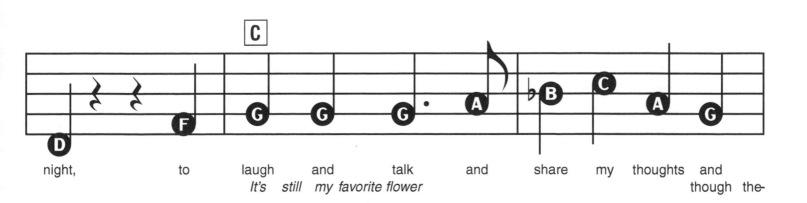

night,   to   laugh   and   talk   and   share   my   thoughts   and
It's   still   my favorite flower   though the-

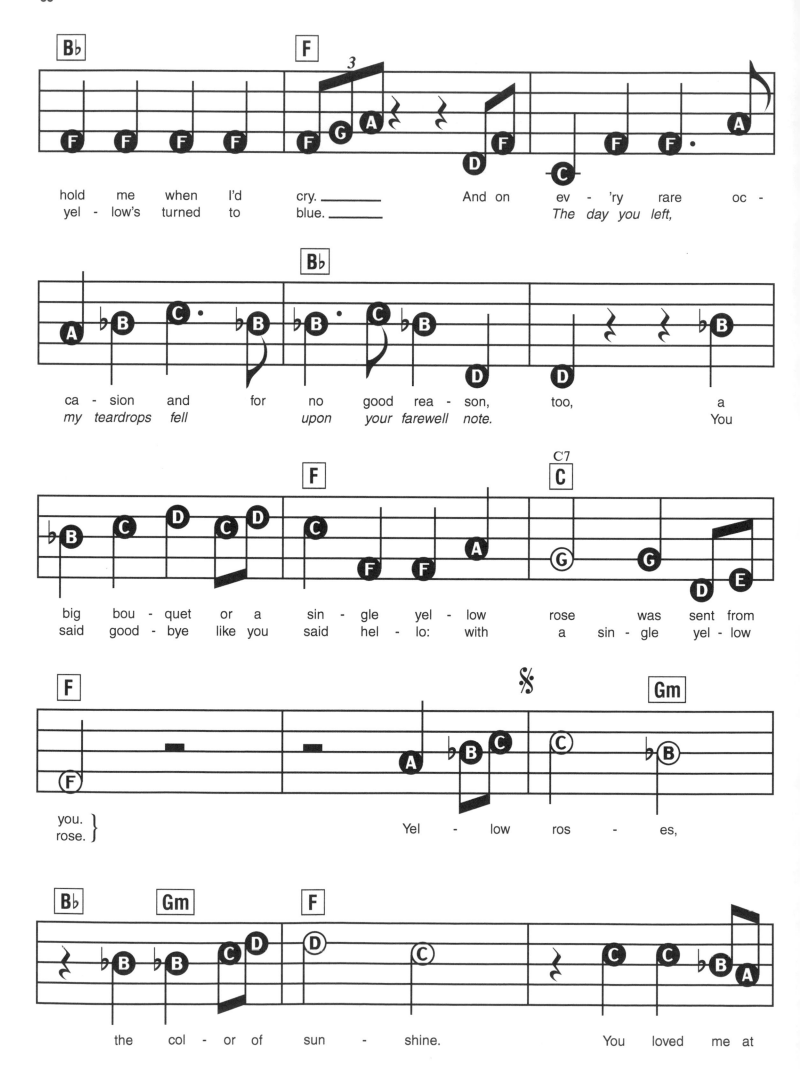

59

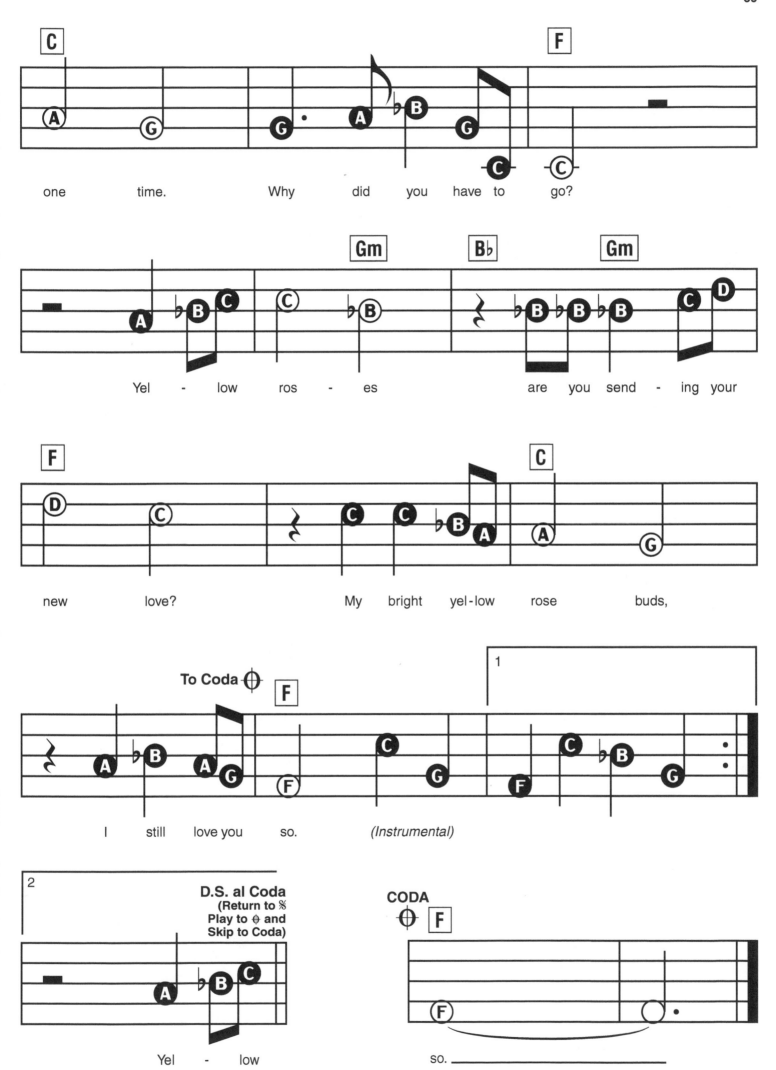

Please Don't Stop Loving Me

Registration 4
Rhythm: Country Pop or Fox Trot

Words and Music by Dolly Parton
and Porter Wagoner

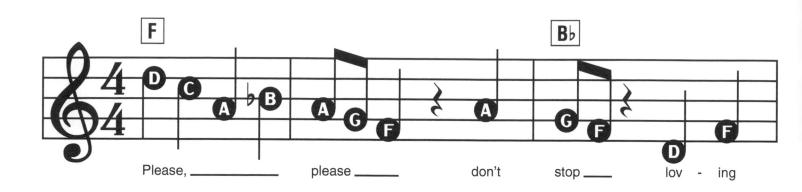

Please, _____ please _____ don't stop ____ lov - ing

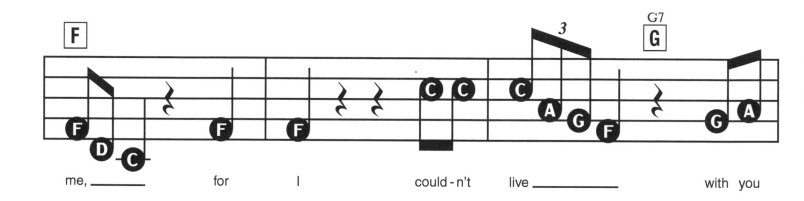

me, _____ for I could - n't live _____ with you

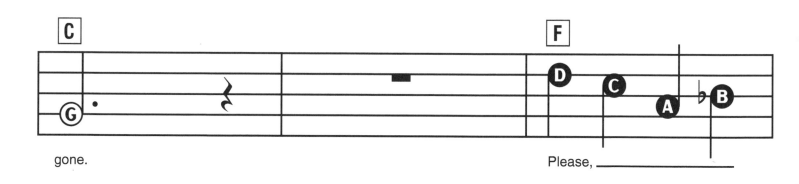

gone. Please, _____

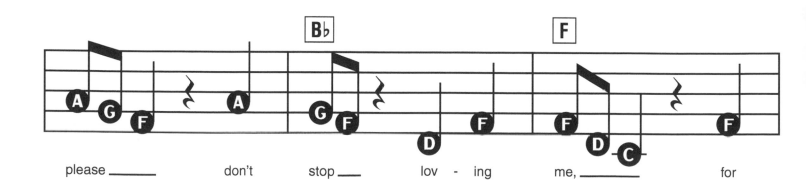

please _____ don't stop ____ lov - ing me, _____ for

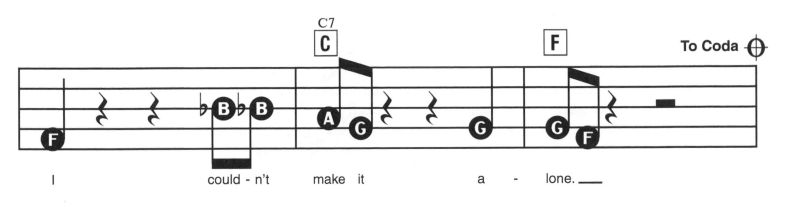

I could-n't make it a - lone. __

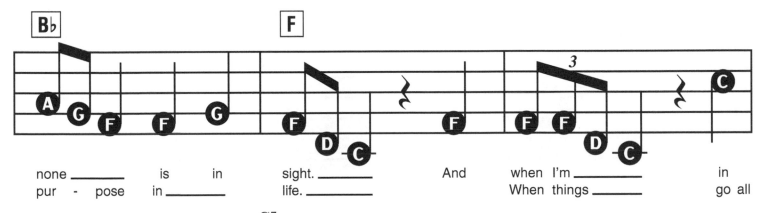

You bring __ me the sun - shine __ when
You're __ my in - spir - a - tion, my

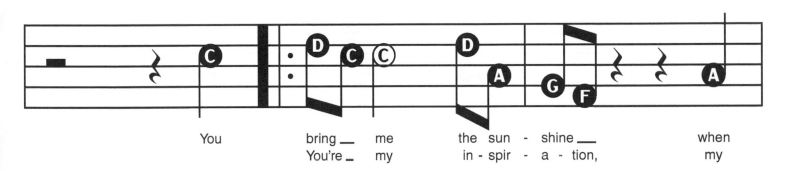

none _____ is in sight. ____ And when I'm _____ in
pur - pose in ___ life. ____ When things _____ go all

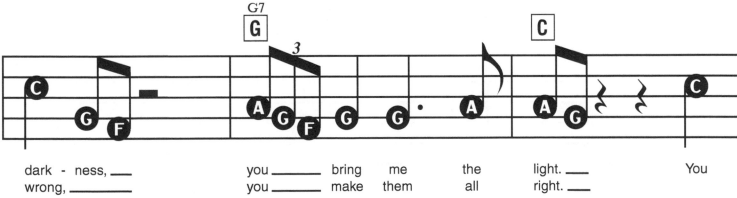

dark - ness, __ you __ bring me the light. __ You
wrong, ____ you __ make them all right. __

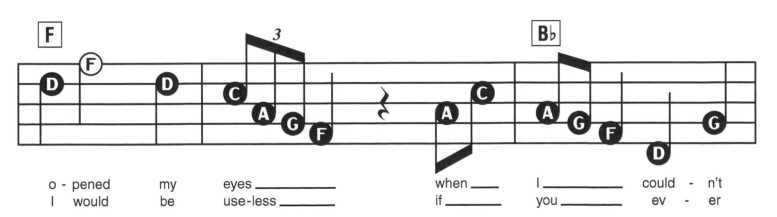

o - pened my eyes _____ when __ I _____ could - n't
I would be use-less ____ if ____ you ____ ev - er

62

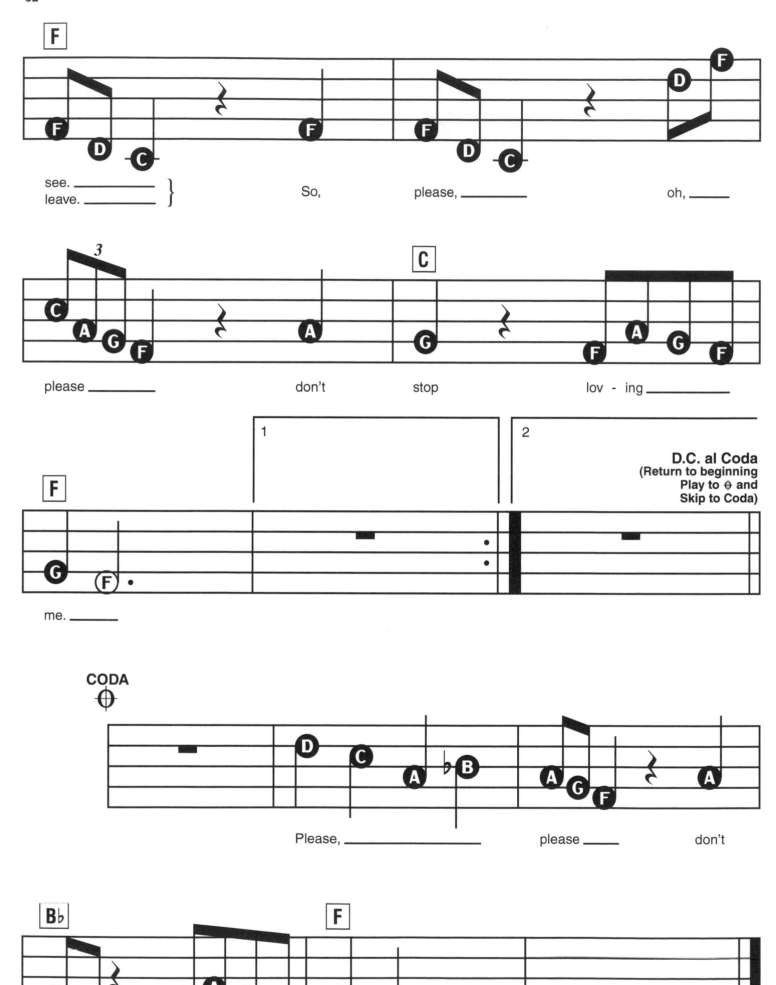

see. _____
leave. _____ }

So,   please, _____   oh, _____

please _____   don't   stop   lov - ing _____

1   2

D.C. al Coda
(Return to beginning
Play to ⊕ and
Skip to Coda)

me. _____

CODA
⊕

Please, _____   please _____   don't

stop _____   lov - ing _____   me. _____